GHETTO SHANGHAI

GHETTO SHANGHAI

by

Evelyn Pike Rubin

FOREWORD BY JUD NEWBORN

Evelyn Pike Rubin

SHENGOLD PUBLISHERS, INC.
NEW YORK

ISBN 1-887563-63-6
Library of Congress Catalog Number: 00-135062

Copyright © 1993, 2000 by Evelyn Pike Rubin
Second Edition

Published by Schreiber/Shengold Publishers, Inc.
51 Monroe Street, Suite 101
Rockville, MD 20850

Printed in the United States of America

Dedicated to my children, Marilyn, Sheldon
Doreen and Sheryl
and to my grandchildren

In memory of my beloved parents
Benno Popielarz, who would not see the evil,
Rika Nelken Popielarz, who did, and took action.

May they rest in Peace
זכרונם לברכה

PREFACE

Ghetto Shanghai is a personal narrative of survival in Japanese occupied Shanghai during World War II.

This is virtually hidden history. During my years as a public speaker at various gatherings, I was amazed at how few people knew of the approximately 18,000 refugees from Nazi-occupied Europe who had found sanctuary in the Orient.

I have tried to tell the story of Jewish refugees, transplanted by circumstances into an alien culture, and to describe in some detail their day-to-day existence. They lived through years of deprivation in the ghetto, and yet, they were among the lucky ones, the survivors.

To this I have added the story of our experiences in the forty-odd years we have lived in the United States. When I give a talk about Shanghai, people always want to know "then what happened?" Here is the answer.

This is a factual story. The only embellishment is the historical background, which I have added for the assistance of the reader.

E. P. R.

Table Of Contents

FOREWORD

The Holocaust was so unprecedented in form, so cataclysmic in its effects, that it irrevocably altered the lives of those it touched—and often in ways that were totally unpredictable. Who would have thought, for example, that an upper middle class Jewish girl from a staid Central European city like Breslau would end up coming of age imprisoned in a ghetto run by, of all people, the Japanese, and in so exotic a locale as Shanghai?

And yet this was exactly the fate of Evelyn Pike Rubin. Like other Jews throughout Europe when given the least opportunity, Rubin and her family faced the Nazi onslaught with remarkable resourcefulness. By taking the uncertain route to occupied China, she and approximately 18,000 other determined refugees came up with a solution to the problem of survival that was as creative as it was desperate.

• • •

The Jews of Germany had experienced a period of deceptive calm following the passage of the notorious Nuremberg Race Laws in 1935. But in 1938 Nazi anti-Jewish measures suddenly increased with disorienting speed. First came the Nazi annexation of Austria, the *Anschluss*; in the course of a single day, Austrian Jews lost their entire civil rights. Acts of violence and public humiliation followed, sending thousands to foreign embassies in search of immigration visas and asylum.

On November 9, 1938, the Jews of Germany found themselves swept up in the violence of *Kristallnacht*—that vast, nation-wide pogrom which, according to Yad Vashem, left as many as 1,400 synagogues and 7,500 businesses destroyed, 100 Jews dead and an additional 30,000 imprisoned for weeks or even months in Nazi concentration camps. These brutal events marked a turning point in the unfolding history of the Holocaust. Before this, some German Jews might still have harbored the hope of living in Nazi Germany, albeit as second-class citizens. But the events of *Kristallnacht* made clear that the vibrant thousand-year old German Jewish community had come to a dead end.

Jews explored every possibility for escape in their efforts to save themselves, from the creation of their own safe havens in Shanghai and elsewhere, like Evelyn Pike Rubin's family, to illegal immigration in derelict ships bound for Palestine. At home they continued welfare efforts and vocational retraining. But the year 1938 was marked by one other key event, one which would strain the hopes of all those who realized that Jewish efforts could not succeed alone— that the only real chance for Jewish rescue lay within the hearts and hands of the civilized world.

During the summer just prior to *Kristallnacht*, the nations of the world had gathered in Evian, France in search of a solution to the Jewish refugee crisis, which had grown in great proportion since the *Anschluss* with Austria in March. Commenting on the prospects of the conference, *New York Times* columnist Anne O'Hare McCormick wrote, "It is heartbreaking to think of the queues of desperate human beings around our consulate in Vienna and other cities waiting in suspense for what happens in Evian. But the question they underline is not simply humanitarian. . . . It is a test of all civilization."

The nations of the world would not rise to that test. Although several had previously accepted refugees, it now appeared as if they had reached the limits of their sympathy. Britain refused outright to discuss Palestine; the U.S.A. would permit no debate over its stringent quota system. Australia announced that "as we have no real racial problem, we are not desirous of importing one." And several Latin American nations issued a joint statement avowing their unwillingness to accept any "traders or intellectuals." Thus the 29 nations at Evian provided a first intimation of what the world's future response would be to the worsening plight of Europe's Jews. With few exceptions, they would offer them nothing.

• • •

As Evelyn Pike Rubin's narrative relates, for those German and Austrian Jews desperate to escape but entirely without hope of obtaining foreign entry visas, the Shanghai solution proved a god-send for in that city no visas were required.

The harsh but welcome salvation Rubin found in the remote Shanghai ghetto represents a chapter of the Holocaust that is little known. For this reason alone, her narrative deserves our attention. Written with the same freshness and immediacy that she brings to her popular lectures, Rubin's story is also filled with color, poignance and humor—another reason why it will appeal, not unlike Anne Frank's gentle diary, to readers of all ages.

Jud Newborn

ACKNOWLEDGMENTS

Had it not been for the support of numerous caring people, *Ghetto Shanghai* would never have been written.

First and foremost the book is a tribute to my mother who always impressed upon me: *Never forget where you came from—never forget what happened to our people*! The hundreds upon hundreds of original documents and photographs that she compiled (only about one percent of which are included in this book), authenticate Jewish life in pre-Hitler and Nazi Germany, as well as in Shanghai. As a realist, she was afraid that history would pass us by—she tried to ensure that this would not happen. Consequently, this enabled me to "tell it like it is."

Special thanks go to Dr. Jud Newborn, a cultural anthropologist and Holocaust scholar, who not only spent many hours giving me advice and ideas, but who was also kind enough to write the foreword. Dr. Newborn is the co-author of *Shattering the German Night: The Story of the White Rose*.

Dr. David Kranzler, author of *Japanese, Nazis and Jews*, and Rabbi Marvin Tokayer, author of *The Fugu Plan*, were most helpful with some of the statistics, names and historical data. They gave me their time and expertise and for this I am grateful.

Thank you to Jacqueline Wolf, author of *Take Care of Josette*, who told me not to give up—some day the book would be published.

Laura Margulies, as an involved and caring staff member of the Joint in Shanghai, gave me some behind-the-scenes insight of the difficult conditions under which she labored when I visited her in Teaneck, New Jersey just a few years ago.

Many thanks to my publisher, Moshe Sheinbaum, and my excellent editor, Ann Finlayson. Her perception of our travels as refugees in the Orient is absolutely amazing, and her research of additional historical data enhanced this narrative for the reader.

Ruth and Isidore Banchik, Bessie and Harry Broadwin, Lillian and Gerard Landsberger, Anne and Rogers Silverman—you reached out to me during an unforgettable time of crisis.

My appreciation to so many others whose unwavering friendship sustained me during some difficult years. Lenny Berger of blessed memory, and Sorell Berger Balaban, Carolyn Carlin, Eve and Hank Conston, Frances and Martin Dinhofer, Ronnie Eigles of blessed memory and Dave Eigles, Norma and Hank Eigles, Dell and Harry Herts, Susie Kushner Lipsey and Rabbi Eugene Lipsey, Molly and Louis Pollack, Zelda Rand of blessed memory, Hilda Rosenthal of blessed memory and Ralph Rosenthal, Frances and Jack Slovis, Natalie Vale, members of my French group and synagogue, Edythea Ginis Selman, who urged me to write the book before I ever thought of it, and many more kind people.

It was the gift of a computer from my wonderful loving and supportive husband Lenny, that "put the show on the road." His invaluable critique was only surpassed by his unwavering commitment to my ideals.

And last, but certainly not least, my dear children, whose combined efforts provided the impetus. Marilyn gave me much needed confidence; Sheldon got me started with an electric typewriter; Doreen's invaluable salesmanship allowed me to continue; and Sheryl's legal expertise was "the icing on the cake" for the finale.

Evelyn Pike Rubin

e-mail: evandlenrubin@aol.com

PROLOGUE

January 30, 1933. Adolf Hitler had just been elected Reichskanzler, Chancellor of Germany. Martial music blared from the radio. From the streets came the noises of a mob gone wild, thousands screeching "*Sieg Heil.*" Vati rushed into the closet and took out the German flag, the republic's red-gold-and-black flag, which we had always displayed from our window on national holidays, and unfurled it. He was a member of the Sozialdemokratische Partei, the Social Democrats, and was very proud of his flag. He opened up the library window and stuck the flagpole in its slot. "Rika, come look," he shouted. My mother ran to the window and stepped back, horrified.

"Benno," she pleaded, "you must take this flag down right away."

"But why?"

"Can't you see what's all around you? Everyone else is displaying the *Hakenkreuze!*"

"So what?" he countered. "I have just as much right as they have to fly my country's flag. They are nothing but a bunch of brownshirted hooligans."

I looked down from the balcony at the streets filled with people. I was too young to understand what was going on, but I knew that there was excitement in the air—and something else too. I remember feeling uneasy. All of a sudden, there was a pounding on the door.

"Now, look what you've done," quavered Rika. "The Nazi bully boys have come for us."

"I have my rights," Vati retorted hotly. "I fought for this country, I was wounded defending the country, I was decorated by the Kaiser himself—they can't do anything to me." Benno went to open the door, and a gentleman in a black coat rushed in.

"Oh, *Herr Himmelfarb, wie geht es Ihnen? Kann ich Ihnen eine Tasse Kaffee anbieten*" offered my mother. For it was our Jewish landlord, whom we knew quite well, and Mutti thought it only proper to offer him a cup of coffee.

Mr. Himmelfarb waved away the suggestion. "*Bitte*, Herr Popielarz," he begged, "take that flag down."

"Never," asserted Vati. "That's my flag—the official flag of the German Republic. I am not taking that flag down."

However, he finally capitulated, when the Brown Shirts threatened to set the building on fire. "Let us leave Germany right now, Benno," pleaded Mutti, "there is no place for us here any longer."

"Oh, nonsense," Vati scoffed. "This madman cannot last! We are living in the most civilized, in the most cultured country on earth. The German people will never let it happen. Let's just wait it out." Accustomed to Vati's common sense and courage, Mutti reluctantly agreed. Little did any of us realize how drastic the consequences would be.

After the Nazis boycotted Jewish stores and businesses in April, 1933, the *Zentralausschuss der deutschen Juden für Hilfe und Aufbau* was founded to support community functions and aid in retraining for and facilitating emigration. These stamps are the receipts of parents' monthly contributions. (Information provided by Leo Baeck Institute.)

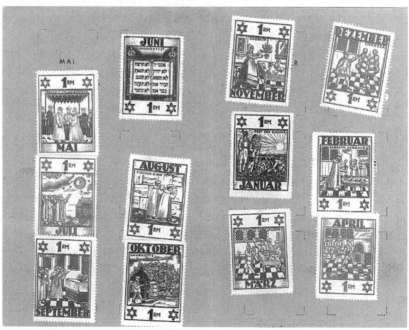

PART I

The Beginning of the End
1930–1939

The Popielarz family—Breslau 1930.

Chapter 1

Breslau (now Wroclaw)

I had been born three years earlier, on July 31, 1930, at Höfchenstrasse 31. In later years, Mutti loved to tell me the story. She and Vati had made reservations in the hospital, but, when the labor pains started, it was already too late to take her there.

Vati was so excited that immediately after Mutti was delivered, he rushed right out to the *Standesamt* to register the birth.

"I have a little girl," he whooped with joy. He filled out the necessary registration forms. The baby's name would be Evelyn Renate Popielarz. (Mutti had always liked the name Evelyn, especially the English spelling of it.) He handed the form to the official. Oh, no, he was told, you cannot register a foreign name in Germany. "Evelyn" was unacceptable. Vati rushed home to Mutti. "What do we do?" he asked her. Mutti, always the practical thinker, had a solution. Why not just Germanize the name to "Eveline," and everyone would be satisfied. Vati rushed back to the *Standesamt*, asked for a new form, and now proudly filled in the name "Eveline Popielarz," daughter of Rika Popielarz, née Nelken, and Benno Popielarz, German army veteran.

When he arrived home, Mutti took one look at the birth certificate. "Benno," she wailed, "you left out 'Renate.' Remember, we wanted Renate as her middle name."

"You're right," said Vati. "I'll go right back and have them correct it." However, when he returned to the *Standesamt*, the official pompously told him that the correction could not be made quite so simply. He would have to apply for a new certificate, which would take weeks to be approved (after all, the original certificate had already been stamped and recorded and would have to be voided), and he would have to pay a large fee in addition. Vati went home to discuss this with Mutti, and they decided it wasn't worth the bother, I would have no middle name. Five years later, I had no choice when the Nazis forced one on me.

My parents now decided to move to larger quarters. They found a beautiful seven-room apartment at Charlottenstrasse 24, a modern apartment building, just ten minutes away from their place of business on Lothringerstrasse. It had a beautiful marble staircase and an open elevator cage.

When you opened the huge oak door to our apartment, you saw a large foyer, covered with a thick-pile Persian carpet. On the left was a tremendous kitchen, with two stoves and two sinks, one each for dairy and meat. Right off the kitchen were two rooms: the pantry and the quarters of Martha, our blond maid, who had been hired to take care of me while my parents went to business. Edith was our everyday cook and Maria the daily cleaning woman.

To the right of the foyer was the drawing room, a fairly large salon containing our library. The carved columns of the bookcases circled two sides of the room, and the shelves reached all the way up to the high ceiling. Two large oil paintings hung on the far wall. A large walnut desk stood in front of the heavily draped window, and next to it were two dark brown leather club chairs. A Louis XIV curio cabinet and a gramophone were on the far side of the room. The rug, also Persian, had a deep red design. The curio cabinet contained Meissen and Rosenthal knick knacks and our demi-tasse sets. I was not allowed into that room when my parents were out, and at other times, it was always "look, but don't touch." My fondest memory of that room is taking a tube of toothpaste and spreading it all around the costly rug. Even though I recollect distinctly my mother's shocked expression when she saw what I had done, and I was severely chastised, I do not remember the punishment meted out.

Beyond that was my bedroom. It was not very large. All the furniture was white, as well as the area rug, and all the toys were on shelves. There was also a little cot in the room so that Martha could sleep with me when I was sick. Next to this room were the two guest rooms.

The dining room contained a large oak table and could seat twenty-four guests. Our Blaupunkt radio was right next to the telephone, which was also connected to the office phone. I still remember the telephone number, 31258, for it was customary to answer the phone with one's number. I was trained, at a very early age, to answer the phone and say, *"Dreihundertzwölfachtundfünfzig"* in one breath.

The radio was soon to become a focal point in the room. I found it very boring, for whenever I entered the room, my parents were glued to it, listening to the news. The news seemed to consist of someone screaming so loud it was hard to understand what he was saying. Much later, I realized it was a man named Adolf Hitler.

Our balcony was just beyond the dining room. It was often used for outdoor entertaining during the summer months. The apartment faced a corner, and from that balcony we had a view of three streets, and a little park.

Mutti was in the paper and twine business with offices and warehouse at Lothringerstrase 10. The firm's logo, *RIPO* (a combination of **RI**ka **PO**pielarz), was prominently displayed at the entrance. Before my mother's marriage, the firm's name had been *RIKA NELKEN*. The warehouse opened into a tremendous courtyard, where the paper-cutting machinery, piles of paper, and balls of twine were kept. The offices were above the warehouse. My mother, of course, had her own office, and even though she had the necessary office help, she liked to do almost everything by herself. She even wrote her own briefs when she had a legal case pending. She had a lawyer, of course, Herr Rechtsanwalt (attorney) Dr. Pinkus who translated these briefs into "legalese," and the team of Rika Popielarz and Dr. Pinkus never lost a case. (He, and his wife and seven children were to perish in Auschwitz.)

Mutti had founded her business in 1916, a few years after the death of her father. Avrohom Nelken, born in Breslau in 1848, was a devoutly religious man. He died in October 1911 during the festival of *Sukkoth*, the Jewish Feast of Tabernacles. A small *sukkah*, or hut, had been erected on the porch, and in it Avrohom and his family would eat all their meals during the eight-day festival. Avrohom would also sleep there. He had been suffering from gout the last few years, and the doctor had advised him against sleeping in the *sukkah* this year, for in October it was already damp and chilly. But he would not listen to the doctor. He felt it was more important to observe ritually this Biblical festival.

Just that year, the family had finally gotten permission from the landlord to install a telephone. He had complained, "It will make a hole in the wall, and then how am I going to rent this apartment if you should move?" But they just had to have this one luxury in case the doctor or an ambulance would have to be summoned during the night.

This was to be his last holiday celebration. He had a cold which developed into pneumonia. He died in his daughter Erika's arms, my Mutti, but not before extracting a difficult promise from her. "Rifkele, my child," he pleaded, "promise me that you'll only marry a man who'll be a *Shomer Shabbos*, a Sabbath observer." Erika promised her father that she would abide by his wish. It was a promise not without its consequences. It now limited her prospects.

(A Sabbath observer does not only have to abide strictly by the laws of *kashruth*, consuming kosher food only, but has to adhere to the restrictions of no work, no riding, no telephoning, no electricity, no smoking, not only on the Sabbath, but also on all the Biblical festivals.)

After her father's death, Erika continued caring for her mother. She was finally engaged to a wonderful man, a Sabbath observer, just as she had promised her father. Her brothers, Samuel and Henoch, as well as her sisters, Frieda and Paula, had gotten married. Moritz and Leo had gone off on their own.

Germany was then embroiled in the Great War, and all the young men had gone off to the front, as had Erika's fiancé. When she received the sad news that the young man had been killed, she realized that she'd have to strike out on her own. It was setting a pattern for Erika's life that was to be repeated more than once.

She decided to follow in the footsteps of her brothers, Moritz and Leo, who had gone into the paper business. Moritz was now living in Berlin and Leo was in charge of the Breslau branch. Erika was going to start her own business in Breslau—paper and twine. To learn the trade, and to overcome her brothers' skepticism of a woman going into business, she started as a door-to-door commission salesman for her brothers, and was successful so quickly that within a year, in 1916, she was in business under her own name: Rika Nelken. She had shortened her name to two syllables.

There was never any competition with her brothers—they worked with each other.

In 1918 the armistice was signed to end "the war of wars." Kaiser Wilhelm abdicated, and the Weimar Republic was established in 1919, with its first president, Friedrich Ebert. He was followed in

1925 by Field Marshal Paul von Hindenburg, an elderly war hero. All were hoping for the good times to come back, but it was not to be. Inflation was rampant; prices skyrocketed so high that a loaf of bread at one time cost one million marks. A former housepainter, with a little mustache, all of a sudden became popular in Munich spouting anti-Semitism by blaming all the ills that had befallen Germany, as well as the Versailles Treaty itself, on the Jews. Yet, despite all that, Rika's business prospered.

Once all the young men who had survived the war had returned from the front, Rika was hoping, once again, to find a husband. Her prospects were slim. She had promised her father that she would only marry a Sabbath observer, and she was not going to break that promise. In addition, anyone who was to attract Rika Nelken had to be cultured, well educated, worldly, and have a sense of humor. That was a tall order.

Even though she had misgivings, she got married in 1921 to a young man whom one of her friends had introduced her to. This marriage was an immediate disaster. Her husband had a nervous breakdown within a year, and Rika gave birth to a stillborn child, after which the marriage was annulled. She was now resigned to continue in her business career.

One of the extracurricular groups that she belonged to was a Zionist athletic club. She would frequent the gym quite often and go to the dances. In March 1928, to celebrate the festival of Purim, commemorating the Jewish victory over the wicked Haman, her group was sponsoring a masked ball. Rika decided to go, looking dashing in a riding costume with boots and a whip.

Rika realized she was already past the so-called acceptable marriage age, three months before she had celebrated her thirty-sixth birthday. Nevertheless, her attention was drawn to a very handsome man in the corner of the room, dressed as a soldier. He was talking to a few people, who were all laughing and enjoying themselves, and Rika walked over to the group, intrigued. Then she too had to laugh. The young man's lips weren't moving, yet words seemed to come from a distant corner of the room—why, he was a ventriloquist! Benno Popielarz, he introduced himself to her, could he have the pleasure of the next dance?

Chapter 2

Benno Popielarz was born on June 6, 1897, in Jarotschin, Provinz Posen (Jarocin, Poznan), to a wealthy, landowning family. He and his brother Leo had lacked nothing that money could buy. Benno had attended gymnasium, graduated with honors, and then, like so many patriotic Germans, had enlisted in the German Army at the outbreak of the Great War. As a Jew he could not become an officer and was therefore given the rank of corporal in a "grenadier" unit. Kaiser Wilhelm II had decorated him, like so many others, with the Iron Cross Second Class, for his bravery in protecting the German *Vaterland*. He cherished this medal all his life.

At the battle of Verdun, he was badly wounded and became a prisoner of war of the French. Shell-shocked and temporarily deaf, he had recuperated in the *Lazerett* (prison hospital). He had always been a ladies' man, and he became very friendly with the nurses, so that, by the time of the armistice, he spoke fluent French.

His war injuries had left Benno with a weak stomach and a penchant for cigarettes, and a shocking memory of a particular battlefield incident. At Verdun, he had found himself face to face with a young French

Document stating that Benno Popielarz was issued the Medal for Wounded in Black, on May 1, 1918.

soldier. The two boys raised their muskets and simultaneously pulled the triggers. Just before losing consciousness from his stomach wound, Benno heard the mortally wounded Frenchman utter "Shema Yisroel," the Jews' holiest prayer. He had killed a fellow Jew! Profoundly traumatized, he was troubled by this episode for the rest of his life.

When Benno came home to Jarotschin, he found that Provinz Posen had become part of Poland in 1919. He had fought for his country and his country had been taken from him. His parents, who had had their roots in Jarotschin for generations, found themselves uprooted. They received the official *Optionsurkunde* in the mail. Now they had a choice of nationality. They could leave their home, many of their possessions, and a way of life that had been very comfortable, and move to the nearest German town. This would allow them to retain their German citizenship. Or, they could stay, and become Polish citizens under an unfamiliar regime. They opted to remain German and moved to Glogau (Glogow), a suburb of Breslau.

Rika knew she had finally met the man of her dreams. He fit all the "necessary" qualifications. He was handsome, intelligent, and cultured, had impeccable manners, was a real Beau Brummel in clothes, a Zionist just like her, never married, a marvelous dancer and, as far as she knew, a Sabbath observer. She brought him home to her mother, who thought he was absolutely charming. Even though Benno was Rika's junior by six years, this never bothered either of them. A few months later they were engaged. Rika gave Benno a beautiful gold pocket watch as an engagement gift; he gave her a splendid diamond ring. Years later the Nazis got the ring, but Benno was allowed to keep the watch.

They were married in Moritz Nelken's Berlin apartment on January 29, 1929. After a long honeymoon in Vienna, they returned to Breslau.

My parents' Vienna
honeymoon, February 1929.

Chapter 3

Rika and Benno made their home in Rika's spacious apartment at
31 Höfchenstrasse, and Benno became the sales manager for his
wife's business.

However, it was my mother who dispatched the salesmen, made
the calls to the customers, and did the buying. She could twist a little
piece of twine between her fingers, or hold a small piece of paper in
her hand, and tell you exactly the weight, strength, quality, and in-
gredients. It was a touch she never lost. My father did help with some
of the selling, but he was mainly her assistant. This was many years
before Women's Lib, but this did not seem to bother him. He had a
great respect for her innate business sense and deferred to her in all
business matters.

Omama Miriam, Mutti's mother, lived in a furnished apartment a
short distance from us, and we would usually visit her on Saturday
afternoons. I was just a little over two years old when she passed

away—during *Sukkoth,* just like her husband, Avrohom, yet I still have hazy memories of sitting on her lap and laboriously buttoning and unbuttoning a sweater that she always wore when I came to visit. Because it used to get dark rather early in the fall, the room was usually quite gloomy. I remember it as very large and her sitting on a rocking chair by the window.

Omama Therese, whom we called Omi, and Opapa Sally (pronounced Zahlee), my father's parents, also lived close by. Opapa died in 1932, about the same time as Omama Miriam, which made Omi Therese my sole surviving grandparent.

Omi had a nephew living with her, but my parents did not feel that this was sufficient protection for her, in view of the prevailing uneasiness and the upcoming November elections. So, Omi and Joseph came to live with us in our two guest rooms.

Joseph's parents had died when he was a little boy, and Omi, his aunt, had raised the young orphan. He had been wounded during the war and remained psychologically scarred. Now in his forties, he was still unmarried. He was a math genius and had a tremendous photographic memory. Today, his condition would probably be diagnosed as "idiot savant."

But Joseph was a lot of fun. He used to play games with me, laughed a lot, and would run with me and take me for walks in the park. He told me stories, taught me card tricks, and how to play checkers and dominoes, and how to roll marbles.

Chapter 4

It was midnight when our doorbell rang. It woke up the whole household. The Nazis! went through everyone's head. Who else would ring the bell at such a late hour? Martha went to the door and asked who was there, and we heard a voice from outside: "Hurry up. It's me, Leo."

"Leo," echoed Mutti. "I might have known." Her brother Leo was a little bit eccentric, despite having become a successful businessman, and often did the unexpected. "Let him in, Martha."

The door was opened, and in he strode in great agitation. "I have only a minute—the chauffeur is waiting downstairs with the motor running."

"Chauffeur? Motor running? Is this another one of your crazy escapades?" demanded Vati.

But for once Uncle Leo was dead serious. "I am leaving Germany—right now. Hans is driving me to Switzerland, and from there I am going to the land of *Liberté, Egalité, Fraternité*," he said excitedly. "To France, to Paris. This is the end for Jews in Germany. France is free, it is a place of refuge. Why don't you all pack and come with me right now?"

I saw my parents exchange glances. I was cowering nearby, wondering why is he leaving in such a hurry? Why does he want us to go with him? I didn't want to leave my toys, my friends, my beautiful little room.

To my relief, Mutti finally sighed and said, "No, Leo, not us. But if you must leave, *geh gezunderheit*," using a Yiddish expression.

Uncle Leo argued a bit more, then threw up his hands, said a hasty good-bye, and left.

"I always told you he was a *meshuggener*," Vati whispered. However, Mutti wasn't too sure. Perhaps, this time, her unconventional brother wasn't so crazy after all.

A month later, we had more visitors. Mutti's nephew, Ruben Beatus, her sister Frieda's son, his wife Rika, and their three children had given up their home in Nürnberg and stopped off in Breslau to say good-bye to us. They were going to Palestine.

We prepared a large farewell dinner for them, not knowing if we were ever going to see them again. What I particularly remember about that dinner is the spinach. The children, of course, always ate separately from the adults. The vegetable was spinach, which I detested, and I refused to eat it. Mutti came into the room. "You have to eat your spinach," she said. "Look how nicely your cousins are eating theirs." I reluctantly ate it and promptly threw it up all over the room. I never went near spinach again.

There seemed to be a constant parade of relatives and friends stopping by to bid farewell to us as they emigrated to various places. Aunt Paula, Mutti's other sister, her husband and children, also came to say good-bye. They too were going to Palestine.

Vati still thought everyone was overreacting. "It will pass. . . ." He really felt that this craziness that had gripped his beloved *Vaterland* was a temporary thing. In the past, Jews had known many bitter times, many savage pogroms, and they had come to an end eventually. We had only to wait out these brutal days, and everything would go back to normal.

Chapter 5

Hitler was now firmly entrenched as Reichskanzler, and the German people were jubilant. It was also time for me to start nursery school. My parents picked a very fine Jewish nursery school for me. However, I was not happy there. As an only child, I guess I had been spoiled. All of a sudden other children were getting attention from someone, in this case the teacher. I reacted by biting some of the children.

Mutti was called to the school and asked to take me home. She found another nursery school for me. There were fewer children there, and I liked it better.

Im Städtlein wo ich wohne
Ist Breslau wohlbekannt,
Es liegt am Oderstrome,
Im liebsten Schlesigerland.

Dort wohnt mein Vati, Mutti,
Mein' Schwester, Brüderlein,
Dort ist mein Kindergarten
Da geh' ich spielen fein.

(In my little township/Breslau is well-known/It lies on the River Oder/In my beloved Silesia./There live my Vati, Mutti/My sister, little brother/There is my Kindergarten/Where I love to play.)

This simple little song, describing Breslau's location in Silesia, is one of my fondest memories of that nursery school. I loved to sing it and still remember the tune as if it were yesterday. However, there was another song that we also had to sing, a song with a melody, though beautiful, still sends shivers down my spine today whenever I hear it. It was heard in the streets and continually on the radio. *"Deutschland, Deutschland über alles, über alles in der Welt. . ."* the German national anthem. We were also taught to sing *"Hatikvah"* (The Hope), the Jewish national anthem, expressing the hope of reestablishing the Jewish national homeland in Palestine.

Despite all this, Vati still felt confident. He even decided to take

Father's German driver's license obtained in 1937. Possibly among the last issued to a Jew in Germany.

driving lessons. He passed his test rather quickly and received his license, and now we could rent a car every Sunday and take drives into the countryside. I loved these rides. The car was an open one, so we had to wear motoring hats and goggles, which were still stylish in the thirties in Europe. These were some of our happiest times as a family.

Then one Sunday, an incident brought a stop to our carefree Sundays. We were on one of our outings when all of a sudden there was a loud "bang" and the car skidded to a stop. Vati got out and discovered he had a flat, and changing it would not be easy, because the car was stuck halfway in a ditch.

Vati flagged down a passing truck. The driver said he'd be happy to help us. He pulled the car out of the ditch in no time and helped Vati put on the spare. Just before getting back into his cab, he started kidding around with me: *"Du bist ja ein schönes Kind. Eine echte Arierin, mit deinen blauen Augen und dem blonden Haar.* (You are a pretty child, a true Aryan, with your blue eyes and blond hair.)" My parents had always taught me to be proud of being a Jew, and I didn't want anyone thinking I was this "Aryan," whatever that meant. I foolishly replied, *"Ich bin keine Arierin. Ich bin jüdisch."*

With that he slammed his hat back on and screamed at us, *"Dreckiger Jude. Hätte ich Zeit, dann würde ich Sie in den Graben zurück stossen.* (Dirty Jew, if I had the time I would push you back into the ditch,)" and with that he took off, tires screeching.

I didn't understand what had made him so angry. Before, he had been very polite. And why did he say I was dirty? I looked at my clothes, and they weren't dirty at all. Finally, I decided he must have meant Vati, who had gotten his hands all smudged changing the tire.

Everyone was very subdued as we got back into the car. I heard my parents whispering. They decided, to my great disappointment, no more driving. "What if we were involved in an accident with a Nazi?" I heard Mutti whisper. "No matter whose fault it would be, as Jews we would be blamed." From then on, if we wanted to take a ride, it would be by bus, train, or taxi.

We had always spent part of the summer at Marienbad (Mariancke Lanzna) when Omama Miriam was alive, for the baths did her a lot of good. This year, 1934, my parents decided not to go away till things settled down a little bit. However, they did not want

Last trip to Spindlemühle (or Spindlermühle) 1934, winter resort in Czecho-slovakia, before Nuremberg Laws forbade foreign travel for Jews.

to forego our usual winter vacation in Spindelmühle, in the Sudeten-land section of Czechoslovakia. (Spindelmühle is no longer on the map.)

I vaguely remembered the place from the previous year. My parents had gone skiing, but I was still too young. The big, beautiful hotel we stayed at was at the bottom of the ski slopes. It was a kosher establishment, and my parents and many of their friends would meet there annually.

We had no premonition that 1934 would be our last winter vacation in Czechoslovakia, or anywhere else.

When we got back to Breslau, I started ice skating lessons. Vati was a great skater, and he would take me to the rink every Sunday. As soon as I stopped falling, I started to enjoy the sport, particularly because I was able to spend so much time with my handsome Vati.

Then it was time to take swimming lessons. I was enrolled in classes at the big public swimming pool. I was told to stand at the edge of the pool and lean over. Suddenly I was pushed sharply from behind and fell into the water headfirst. Force, that was the German way of teaching: Obey without question, adhere to all the rules. *Achtung!*

I hated that teacher. The same thing happened the following week. I begged the teacher not to push me in. I thought I was going to drown, and I hated getting chlorine in my nose. Again I was pushed, yet even though Fraülein Hermann was happy with my progress, I was learning the breaststroke, the water still scared me. I didn't mind the swimming—I just hated being pushed in. After a couple of weeks, the teacher decided I was now ready to learn the crawl.

But the following week, when Martha and I arrived at the appointed time for my swimming lesson, we were confronted by a large sign posted at the entrance. Martha read it and seemed taken aback. "Let's go home," she said.

"But Mutti will be angry with me if I don't have my lesson!" I protested.

"Well, we can't go in. They're not letting us go in." She looked at the sign again and shook her head.

"Is that what the sign says?" I asked her.

Martha hesitated, and then, reluctantly, read the harsh words to me: "JUDEN UNERWÜNSCHT (Jews unwanted)."

I was too young to realize what this crude notice implied. I was just glad I wouldn't have to take any more swimming lessons. I wanted to hurry home and tell Mutti.

But at home, before I could utter a word, Martha had taken Mutti aside, and a moment later Mutti came into the room crying. I was so upset, I forgot my good news.

"You poor child," she said to me, and then whispered to herself, "Why are they so afraid of children?"

Afraid of me? Why would anyone be afraid of me? Grownups were really confusing.

But I soon forgot this in the excitement of our upcoming trip. Mutti and I were going to Poland, to see a cousin in Kalisz get married. Vati wasn't interested in weddings, and besides, he had to stay behind to run the business.

It seemed to me like a long train trip, even though it was only sixty-five miles from Breslau. Upon our arrival in Kalisz, we were picked up and driven in a horse and carriage to our destination. That was really exciting. Everyone spoke Polish, and my mother had to make herself understood with the few words of the language she had picked up from Vati and Omama Miriam.

We received a big welcome at our cousins' home. It looked as if the whole world was there to greet us. There was a lot of hugging, kissing, and eating, as well as singing and dancing.

Of course, it was going to be a strictly Orthodox wedding, an affair that was to last seven days. I met loads of relatives I had never seen before—cousins my age I didn't even know existed. They spoke a language that was sort of familiar but not quite. It sounded like German, yet it wasn't. Many years later I realized that this was the first time I had heard Yiddish spoken.

We had planned to stay the whole week, but after two days, we received an urgent telegram from Vati. Come back immediately, he urged. The travel privileges of all German Jews had been suspended, and we might be stranded in Poland. So we packed up and left, to my great disappointment. We were never to see these cousins again.

This new restriction made us virtual prisoners in our own country. We were still permitted to travel within Germany, but no permission was granted for travel outside the country. There went our

Mother's German passport. On first page, note the letter "J" which was in red. Pages 2 and 3 also list author as Eveline Sara Popielarz.

winter skiing vacations to Czechoslovakia. A big red *J* was stamped onto our passports to signify that we were Jewish. We were also deprived of our voting rights and permission to carry firearms, and we had to add proscribed middle names to our existing names.

So that it should never appear like coercion, we had to petition the authorities for permission to add these particular names, All females had to add the name "Sara" and all males the name "Israel," and henceforth were required to use them as middle names. Well, I now had a middle name: Sara.

In spite of these increasingly stringent restriction against Jews, my parents still hoped that the situation was just temporary. We tried to continue living our normal existence under abnormal conditions.

The following Sunday, the weather was nice and brisk. Vati and I dressed in our skating outfits, and we three set out for the public skating rink. I wanted to show off what I could do, so Mutti came along to watch. A crowd was gathered near the entrance to the rink. Something was going on. When we spotted some friends, we asked what was happening. "We're not allowed," they replied.

"What do you mean, not allowed?" I cried in dismay.

They pointed to a sign on the gate, the same ugly sign I had seen at the entrance to the swimming pool: "JUDEN UNERWÜNSCHT."

I started to cry. Why didn't anyone want me to skate? I wanted to know. My parents told me I was too young to understand, but there were bad people who didn't like Jews, and we were Jewish, so they didn't like us. Bewildered and frightened, I took my parents' hands, and we slowly made our way home. No one said a word.

Chapter 6

July 31, 1935. My parents made a big fifth birthday party for me. In September, I would be starting school. No more Kindergarten, the German name for nursery school.

Since the Nürnberg Laws had gone into effect, Jewish children were not admitted to the public schools, but as the child of a war veteran, I was entitled to an exemption. However, my parents decided to send me to a private Jewish school, the Wohlschule, run by Fraülein Wohl, on Lothringerstrasse, down the block from my parents' business.

In Germany, the first day of school was always a very exciting event. Every child received a *Tüte* (literally, "horn"), a large, colorful cardboard package, cone-shaped, usually filled with candy and little gifts. After the school opening, it was customary to picnic in the park so that these *Tüten* could be opened to see what surprises they contained. I had received two such *Tüten*, one from my parents and one from some friends of the family. I was the only one to have gotten two *Tüten*. I felt very superior to the other children.

The classes at the Wohlschule were pretty small, about ten students per class. Till the advent of Hitler, English had been taught at the school, as well as the familiar Latin handwriting. Now it was forbidden to teach English and it was mandatory to teach the German *Sütterlin* script. We were still allowed to have religious instruction, which of course included Hebrew. Here, too, we would sing

First day of school—Breslau 1935.
Author with her two *Tüten*.

33

"Deutschland, Deutschland über Alles. . ." followed by *"Hatikvah,"* at the start of every school day.

I do not have happy recollections of the Wohlschule. Surely it must have been the times. With people starting to emigrate, we not only lost students but teachers as well. As soon as we got used to a new teacher, or started a friendship, the teacher would emigrate, and so would the friends.

Every morning Martha would walk me to school, and every afternoon she would pick me up. On Fridays, my parents would pick me up, for school was over at one o'clock, in time to prepare for the Sabbath.

On Friday, Omi Therese would bake the *challahs*, the braided bread, for the Sabbath. She would always leave me a little piece of dough for braiding, to make little *challahs* for my dolls. How I loved the smell of baking bread, and how delicious it tasted.

After a sumptuous Sabbath dinner in the dining room, the one time during the week when I was allowed to eat with my parents, we would walk to the Storch synagogue, where Mutti and I would sit upstairs in the balcony in the women's section, and Vati would be praying downstairs with the men.

Sometimes Vati would take me downstairs with him, which I thoroughly enjoyed. Somehow the men did not frown on little girls coming down to sit with them.

Martha had been trained to leave certain lights on and then to shut them off before going to sleep for, as Sabbath observers, we could not touch the electric light switches on the Sabbath.

The following morning, we would walk to the synagogue again. I used to enjoy these walks. We would always meet people and stop to chat, and after synagogue services, we would have our cold lunch, and when the weather was nice, we would go to the park. At other times we would either visit friends or have them visit us.

One of my fondest recollections of Vati, always the maverick, is his riding the elevator—strictly forbidden for Sabbath observers. After we walked home from the synagogue, Mutti and I would start walking up the five flights of stairs to our apartment, and there Vati would be, waving to us from the open elevator as he went by. Mutti would shake her head at this naughty performance.

I enjoyed celebrating all the Jewish holidays. Purim was always fun. It celebrated the victory of the Jews in ancient Persia over the evil Haman. All little boys dressed up as either King Ahasuerus, Mordecai (Esther's uncle), or the wicked Haman. Little girls would dress either as Queen Vashti or as Queen Esther. Mutti would make me a little crown by wrapping gold colored paper around cardboard and I was even allowed to wear some of her jewelry.

On Passover, we always had a big seder, and I learned to recite the four questions at a very early age. *"Mah Nishtanah Halailah Hazeh. . . ?* (Why is this night different from all other nights. . . ?)"

All the Passover dishes were stored in the attic, and Omi, Martha and I would go up there to bring them down. Edith's husband used to help us carry them. It was a lot of fun crawling into the attic, with all the dust, and going through the cartons and seeing our suitcases stored there, as well as some unused furniture. I loved eating matzah with butter. The matzoth were round and very crisp. Omi did most of the cooking, and I helped make the matzah balls.

Next would come *Shavuoth*, seven weeks after Passover, when the weather would already be warm, and after synagogue services, we would have our lunch on the terrace.

When *Rosh Hashanah*, the Jewish New Year, came along in the fall, it was time to buy new clothes. I would always get my new fall and winter clothes at that time, but I was not allowed to wear them till we went to the synagogue. It was fun running around the synagogue courtyard with my friends and comparing our new outfits.

Then came *Yom Kippur*, when my parents would fast. I was too young to fast, but Mutti would allow me to skip breakfast, and then Martha would come to pick me up from the synagogue for lunch. The service lasted all day, and usually in the early afternoon, Mutti would take me to visit Omi in her synagogue. It seemed that there were only old people where she prayed. It was a very small *shul*, and there were curtains hung around the railing of the balcony, so that no one could look down at the men, as we were able to do at the Storch synagogue.

Vati used to be very irritable on *Yom Kippur* and was no fun at all. I guess this was because he couldn't smoke. The first thing he did when we came home after the *Ne'ilah* service was to run for a cigarette. Then, all of a sudden he was his old self again.

Sukkoth, the Feast of Tabernacles, commemorating the huts the Israelites lived in during their forty years of wandering in the wilderness after the exodus from Egypt, was the next holiday. I loved going into the temple *sukkah* and seeing the beautiful decorations and smelling the pine branches that were laid across the stakes on the open roof and then participating in the *kiddush*. After services, there would usually be a lot of fruit and cake. Mutti showed me how to make a small *sukkah* out of a shoe box. I would cut a little door at each end and then square holes for the windows. These I would cover with colored cellophane paper. I would fashion a little table and two chairs out of cardboard and then glue candlesticks, made out of twisted tinfoil, onto the table. Next I would place the little braided challahs on the table. I would usually glue paper dolls into the chairs. The top would be covered with small tree branches and little pieces of candy hanging down.

I particularly looked forward to the last day of this eight-day festival, *Simchat Torah*. That is the day when the last paragraph in the Torah, the holy scroll, is read, everyone dances around with the Torah; there is singing, eating, and drinking. The children were all given flags and bags of candy, while everyone rejoiced. I was allowed to take this flag home from the synagogue, but it had to be wrapped up in brown paper, just like Vati's *tallith*, his prayer shawl, and the *Siddur* or *Machsor*, prayer books. We never knew when we would meet a Nazi in the street, so it was safer for us to carry an innocuous package.

Hanukkah, commemorating the victory of the Maccabees over Antiochus Epiphanes and the rededication of the Temple in 165 B.C.E. was celebrated during December. We had a big menorah, and every night another candle would be lighted, one for each of the eight days of the festival. A *Hanukkah* Man would come to our apartment, carrying a big sack with all kinds of presents for me. Years later I discovered that the *Hanukkah* Man was one of Mutti's salesmen. (He and his family perished in the Holocaust.)

Chapter 7

There seemed to be no end to the restrictions on Jews. Hitler had instituted a voluntary *Rentenversicherung*, a social security plan for the self-employed. Mutti had decided to join that plan. After paying into it for two years, it was frozen. She could not withdraw her money, neither could she add to it. Also, Vati's life insurance was frozen.

He now had to admit that it looked as if Hitler was going to be around awhile, and when the edict barring Jews from carrying firearms was instituted, he decided to defy it.

My father had always owned a pistol license and would periodically go target practicing. Now he was told he had to turn in his gun. Instead, he kept quiet, determined to hang on to the weapon. Then, one day, he heard that a business associate had been arrested. The Gestapo had started to make house searches in Jewish homes— for which they did not require a warrant—and had found a licensed pistol that had not been turned in. The man was sent to prison, never to be heard from again. Now Vati didn't know what to do. It was too late to turn in the gun, yet he was afraid to keep it in the house. What if the Gestapo made a house search of our apartment? He could not take that chance.

Vati decided to dismantle the pistol. Every night he and I would go for a walk along the Oder, and every night a piece of the pistol would end up in the river. Mutti told me she did not have a peaceful night till the last piece of that pistol was disposed of.

To add to an already bad situation, I kept getting sick. It seemed that I always had a sore throat and had difficulty swallowing. On a day in early fall, Mutti told me we were going on a special outing and I would be getting a lot of ice cream. I was very excited. I loved ice cream and I also loved riding in a car, something I missed since we no longer went on outings. Also, I was glad of Mutti's attention. Lately, all my parents' time was spent with organizations and contacts that might help us emigrate.

We arrived at a big building at the other end of town and walked into a waiting room, where Mutti said we would be meeting some "very nice people." The "nice people" turned out to be a man and some women wearing white coats, who ushered us into a big room and told me to sit down in a chair. Mutti said not to be frightened, because the doctor was going to make my throat feel all better.

"Doctor," I screamed.

All of a sudden, something was put over my face. I tried to scream, but no sound came out. After what seemed like a few minutes, I was lying on a bed, and my throat hurt terribly. I had had a tonsillectomy. Sure enough I got the promised ice cream, but I was angry with Mutti for not having told me what was going to happen. It would be a week before I wanted to speak to anyone again.

Hanukkah was approaching again, and as usual, I looked forward to the holiday, the lighting of the candles, singing the songs, getting presents and playing the delightful dreidel game. This would be played with a little top that had Hebrew lettering on it. The four letters, *nun* (נ), *gimel* (ג), *hay* (ה) and *shin* (ש), stood for "*Nes Gadol Hayah Sham*" (a great miracle happened there), referring to the miraculous eight-day burning of the Temple oil. Candy would be the prize depending on what letter the dreidel stopped at.

However, just before the holiday, I got sick again. This time it was scarlet fever. I was quarantined in my room, and everyone who came to visit me had to put on a surgical mask and a white gown and wash his hands with disinfectant when leaving. I was thus a prisoner for ten days. All my *Hanukkah* gifts were washed with disinfectant, and those that couldn't be washed were thrown away after I recovered. I never forgot that *Hanukkah* in isolation.

Chapter 8

Spring 1936. My parents were studying Portuguese, hoping to emigrate to Brazil. At the same time, they were exploring other avenues. They bought English language books, hoping to join Mutti's sister, Paula, in Palestine. Then word came that Cuba was accepting Jewish refugees from Germany. Now Spanish was added to my parents' curriculum.

It really did not seem so strange to me to hear all those foreign languages spoken at home. After all, both Omi and Vati spoke Polish, a language Omi would usually use when conversing with her friends—especially if they did not want me to know what they were saying. Then, of course, when Vati got together with his buddies, some of whom had also been POW's in France, they would speak French. Hebrew was the language for prayer. I studied it in school and then heard it in the synagogue. Now it seemed that I heard unfamiliar languages all the time. Would I have to learn to speak another language besides German, I wondered.

Suddenly, Mutti had an idea. Leo was now permanently settled in Paris, where he had established a French branch of the paper-and-twine business on the rue Desnouettes. Perhaps the French government would permit us to join him. Vati, being fluent in French, decided it would be logical for him to go to Paris. He applied for a visitor's visa, and the French approved it, but the Nazis would not let him leave. He could only get a German exit visa if the French approved a permanent residency visa. So Mutti applied, requesting permission to visit her brother, on the pretext that he was all alone in Paris, without family, and quite ill. Surprisingly, the Nazis granted her a temporary exit visa, and off to Paris she went. She left with hope, and returned in despair. The French would not allow us to emigrate to join Leo. We did not know it then, but this denial saved our lives.

In the meantime, Omi had been in correspondence with her sister Rosa, who lived in New York. She had come to the United States as a young girl with her father and had married a young Russian-Jewish immigrant. They had two children and lived in Brooklyn. Omi now wrote her, requesting that she send us an affidavit to emigrate to the United States.

We waited for her reply with bated breath. It was truly our last hope. So far, the Nazis had allowed my parents to continue running their business, although it had dropped off considerably. Many of the Jewish salesmen were emigrating, and some of Mutti's customers stopped doing business with her, because they either didn't want—or were afraid—to buy from Jews. We were unable to sponsor our own affidavit for, in order to do that, money had to be available outside Germany, either in U.S. dollars or British pounds sterling. Our money was all in Reichsmarks (the revalued currency established in 1925), which we were not allowed to take out of Germany. Finally, the long-awaited letter arrived from New York: "Don't you know that America is in a depression? We cannot sponsor you. We do not have the necessary funds to support you." When a sponsor arranged for an affidavit, he had to guarantee that the people he was sponsoring would not become a burden on the government—that is, that either they would be self-supporting or that he, the sponsor, would support them.

Vati wrote back to his aunt that we would be permitted to bring all our furniture and all of our personal possessions. My parents were still young and able to work. However, it was to no avail. Rosa was afraid that she would have to support us.

Chapter 9

Everything that had seemed so secure in my life was now changing. No more visits to the park to play with my friends, who were not allowed out there either. We were not told why, so it was all very mysterious. We still attended each other's birthday parties, which were more like farewell parties, for no one knew if we'd still be in the same place next year. Everyone went around whispering, and when they didn't whisper, all they could talk about was emigration. "Do you know that the Kohns just got a visa to go to America? Did you hear that the Goldbergs are leaving for England?" and so it went. When you met friends or acquaintances in the street they did not greet you with the customary *"Wie geht es Ihnen?* (How are you?)" but rather "when are you leaving and where are you going?"

And then, of course, there were the parades. It seemed as if we had them every single day. I remember the frenzied crowds as they stood with silly, outstretched arms screaming, *"Heil* Hitler *Heil* Hitler! *Sieg Heil!" "Gott segne unseren Führer!"* over and over again, till they were hoarse. It was all very frightening.

If I happened to be out with Martha when a parade went by, I could see that she was not happy stretching out her arm and chanting *"Heil* Hitler" with the mob, but no one was allowed to stand by without saluting. She used to whisk me away as soon as she could.

When I was out with my parents, things were different. Then we did not even go near the parades. As soon as we heard music, we ran into the nearest store or lobby of an apartment house till the parade went by, for Jews were not allowed to give the Nazi salute.

I can still see the Hitler Youth, under the leadership of Baldur von Schirach—cold blooded, unruly young thugs, typical juvenile delinquents—marching down the elegant, chestnut-tree-lined Kaiser Wilhelmstrasse, goose stepping to the tune of the Horst Wessel Lied. Horst Wessel, a little pimp from Munich who became a hero by getting himself murdered by the Communists, had left behind a song which began *"Die Fahne hoch, die Reihen fest geschlossen, SS marschiert im gleichen Schritt und Tritt. . . ."* The Nazis loved it and made it their party anthem.

By now I had become more aware of what was happening, without realizing all the political implications. My blond hair and blue eyes inadvertently protected me from many a Gestapo-Jewish confrontation. I suppose going places with Martha, so typically Aryan, helped also.

Occasionally, on Martha's days off, Vati would have me go to the grocery to buy his cigarettes. Almost all stores now bore the very recognizable legend on their doors: JUDEN UNERWÜNSCHT. I was never challenged, but Mutti was very upset with Vati for sending me.

Chapter 10

Summer 1937. We still had no place to go. We had to stay in the Germany that didn't want us, the Germany of my ancestors, the Germany my father had fought for, and the Germany that my parents had loved.

Then, Vati's brother, Leo Popielarz, informed us that he managed to get papers for Paraguay and that he was leaving immediately with his wife and little daughter, my cousin Lore. It seems that he had accumulated some gambling debts, and he had to run fast. Previously, Vati had bailed him out, always to Mutti's chagrin, but now that our money was frozen, the "well had run dry" for him too. After a long period of time, he wrote to Omi that he had reached Asuncion.

New restrictions. No Aryan females under the age of forty-five were allowed to work in Jewish households. In the eyes of the Nazis, every Jewish male was considered a potential seducer of Aryan women. A Jew having sexual relations with an Aryan was committing the unforgivable *Rassenschande*, pollution of the race.

Martha, who was only thirty-seven years old at this time, was devastated that she had to leave us. She had been with the family since 1930. My parents had been very good to her. As a matter of fact, Mutti told me in later years, she had been carrying on with a chauffeur, and when she became pregnant, Mutti paid for her abortion. That was not easy to arrange in those days, besides being very costly. Martha had been very grateful to Mutti, particularly because she had expected to be fired. Also, she was very fond of me, and this kind of position, because of the times, was not easy to come by anymore. However, she had to obey the law. She ended up being a waitress.

Edith was forty-five years old and was allowed to continue working for us, and so was Maria. We now hired a young Jewish girl who was to take me to school every morning and pick me up after school. She did not sleep in but went home after dinner.

Till Martha was forced to leave us, I would have dinner with her, and sometimes with Omi and Joseph. Now that she was gone, our routine was totally changed. We would wait for Vati and Mutti to come from the office, and we would all have our dinner in the large dining room. Edith would serve and go home after cleaning up.

Uncle Moritz was still running his paper-and-twine business in Berlin. He applied for, and was granted a British visitor's visa. A few months later, he was able to arrange, through some British business associates of his, for his wife Henny, as well as his daughters, fifteen-year-old Lilo and thirteen-year-old Margot, to follow him. They managed to get their valuables, fine furniture, and personal possessions shipped to Manchester where they were to take up residence. The only catch was that Henny had to work as a domestic, while Moritz was interned on the Isle of Man as an enemy alien because he came to England on his German passport. When England declared war on Germany, he was released and joined his family in Manchester.

One morning, my parents stopped by my room as I was getting ready to go to school—an unusual occurrence for them. Wouldn't it be exciting, they asked, if I were to go to England to live with Uncle Moritz, Aunt Henny, and my cousins in Manchester? I thought it was a horrible idea. Where was England? I wanted to know. They showed me on a map. It seemed very far removed from Breslau—an island surrounded by water. Would Mutti and Vati come also? No, they informed me, only children would be allowed to go at present. They might be able to join me at a later time.

I got hysterical. Leave Mutti, Vati, Omi, my friends, everything that was familiar? Go to a strange country, far away, where I couldn't even speak German? And what if Mutti and Vati couldn't come there? What if I never saw them again? The English must be terrible people if they wanted to separate me from my parents. Why wouldn't they let Mutti, Vati, and Omi come also? And live with relatives I barely knew?

"No, I am not going."

"But please, Evelinchen," pleaded Vati, "it will be an exciting trip. You will make new friends, and we will probably be able to see you soon."

"No, no. I am not going without you," I insisted. I was so adamant, they dropped the subject.

It seems that the British government wanted to show the world some humanity, vis-à-vis Nazi anti-Semitism, by accepting transports of Jewish children from Germany and Austria. After being pressured by British Jews, of course, many desperate parents did send their children to England, either to stay with relatives or with strangers who opened their homes to these little refugees. If they were in their teens, they helped with housework or baby-sitting.

Life had now changed drastically for us. No more trips, no more recreation, no more picnics, no more entertaining. My parents went about their business, and I continued attending school. Whenever we turned on our Blaupunkt radio, we heard martial music, the Nazi songs, especially a bloodthirsty ditty they were so fond of singing: "*Wenn's Judenblut vom Messer spritzt dann geht's nochmal so gut*. . . (When Jewish blood flows from the knife then things will be so much better)."

"It is time," Mutti said one evening at dinner, "that we gave up our apartment."

I couldn't believe what I heard. Give up our apartment? Let strangers move in? And where would we live? I couldn't imagine ever living anywhere else.

My parents went looking for a small furnished apartment and made arrangements to sell whatever we could not take with us.

Chapter 11

Spring 1938. the Austrian *Anschluss*. The Nazi horde walked into Austria and was welcomed with open arms:

EIN LAND—-EIN VOLK—EIN FÜHRER
(One Land—One People—One Leader)

We are all one country. We share a language. We shall conquer the world. *Juden raus.* Let's get rid of the Jews, the scourge of society. *Die Juden sind unser Unglück.*

So screamed the headlines. And there was Julius Streicher. The virulent anti-Semite, publisher of the scurrilous, lurid, and obscene rag, DER STÜRMER. It was filled with lies about Jews, as well as vile and pornographic inventions that disgusted even staunch Nazis. And yet many ordinary Germans read it and believed its falsehoods.

A new anti-Semitic edict. All Jews had to deliver up their valuables: precious stones, gold, sterling. Of the flatware, we were each allowed to keep one piece, either a fork, spoon or knife. Of the jewelry, only the gold wedding band, if married, and one gold watch per person. Silver plate, brass, crystal, etc., did not have to be turned in.

I went with Mutti to the *Amt* (bureau) where we had to deliver our valuables: her engagement ring, beautiful pins, bracelets, rings, necklaces. Mutti cried bitterly when she had to give up Omama Miriam's engagement ring. We also had with us Omi Therese's jewelry, brought with her from Jarotschin. She was too upset to come with us. We had ten sterling flatware sets. Dairy, meat, for everyday, for company, for Passover, and then some. Because my parents did a lot of business with the silver factories, selling them tissue paper, they in turn gave us a lot of beautiful gifts around holiday time. It all ended up in Nazi coffers.

One particular sterling set so impressed the clerk who gave us our receipts plus a tiny token sum (so we couldn't say that the Nazis took it from us, we *sold* it to them) that he told my mother he would give her more than the assigned amount if she would not break up the set, which she was entitled to do by holding back one item. She said no. He offered her double, even triple, but Mutti wouldn't budge. Later, when she told Vati the story, she added that even if he had given her the full value of the whole set, she would not have accepted it. He probably wanted the set for himself.

Omi had given me a small gold watch, which I was allowed to keep. Many years later, this little watch would buy food for a whole month. Mutti also had a gold watch, and Vati was allowed to retain the one Mutti had given him in 1928. I still have it. It keeps time to the second and brings back many fond memories.

We walked out of there much subdued and saddened. It was still difficult for me to grasp the idea that people were allowed to steal our things, just because we were Jewish, and that no one could do anything about it.

The next item of business was disposing of the apartment. People came day in and day out, looking at our possessions. The prices we, as Jews, were allowed to charge were mandated by the government. All our beautiful things went for a pittance. Then one day a priest appeared. He was interested in purchasing our library.

He looked over the books and the carved wall-to-ceiling unit. He decided he was going to give us more than the mandated price. Mutti would not accept. How could she be sure he was not a Gestapo agent trying to entrap her?

July 31, 1938, my eighth birthday. My parents had always made big birthday parties for me, and I received many presents. They would ask me to make a list of everything I wanted about a month before my birthday. Then, while I was asleep, they would spread the presents out next to my bed, and when I awoke in the morning, I was barely able to contain myself enough to open them. In fact, I was often so excited about my birthday that I'd wake up in the middle of the night and try to feel the presents next to me and guess what they were.

All of our furniture had already been sold, and everything else was packed. Luckily it was a nice day, and we had the party on the balcony. It was also going to be the last time that I would see many of my friends. Mixed in with the celebration was a lot of sadness. It was the end of an era.

Mutti decided that it would be a good time for Vati to take up a trade. After all, business was slow now, and she could handle it all by herself. She felt that if we were going to emigrate, it would be much easier to make a living in a new land with a trade than by starting a business.

After much discussion, Vati enrolled in a trade school to study typewriter mechanics. Upon completion of the six-month course, he received a certificate.

Our new quarters were very cramped. We kept our bags packed, hoping to find a country that would let us in. Vati had desperately written to the Hebrew Immigrant Aid Society (HIAS) in New York, asking for their help in getting us an American affidavit from his aunt. Finally, they were able to get her to sign all the necessary papers, giving her, in return, a guarantee that the organization would take care of us and we would not be a financial burden to her—or the American government. That summer we received the affidavit. Now, all we had to do was wait for our American visa, and we would be on our way to freedom.

Many of our friends had already received their visas, and we looked forward to joining them in freedom in the *goldeneh medineh*, America. The day the letter arrived, with the return address of the American Consulate in Berlin, was an exciting day indeed. Mutti tore open the envelope. All of a sudden her face fell.

"*Was ist den los?*" cried Vati.

"You won't believe this, but we're on Polish quota, and the quota is filled. We have a long wait ahead of us."

"What do you mean, 'Polish quota,' " exclaimed Vati. "There must be some mistake, we're no more Polish than that *meshuggene* Hitler. I fought in the Kaiser's army. I was decorated by him as a German soldier. What kind of nonsense?"

Unfortunately this nonsense was real. My parents discovered, to their chagrin, that the American quota system, established in 1921, was based on the status of one's birth place from that year on. Because Poznan had become a part of Poland in 1919, Vati and his family, for purposes of immigration to the United States, were placed on the small Polish quota. Had we been on the German quota, we could have left almost immediately.

Despair settled over us. Our last hope was gone. The doors of the world seemed closed to us.

And then we heard about one open door.

Chapter 12

When Hitler annexed Austria in the Spring of 1938, Austrian Jews panicked and tried to emigrate, in a big hurry. Somehow, after some research, they discovered that Shanghai, China, still had an open-door policy. The city allowed anyone in who had the price of a steamship ticket plus board money, which consisted of a particular sum of money, in foreign currency, deposited with the steamship line and held in escrow till the owner's arrival in Shanghai.

Of course word had come to Germany that this was a last resort if no other country would accept us—definitely, a *last* resort, for in 1938, Shanghai was an unknown entity and seemed a terrifyingly strange place to emigrate to. Yet, as other doors closed—slam! slam! slam!—this faraway city began to seem friendlier.

As I walked in the street with my parents, people would stop to tell us that the Hettsteins, the Pinkuses, the Rosens, and others were leaving for Shanghai. Others would say, "*Schanghai, Sie sind ja verrückt. Sie können sich gleich Ihren Sarg mitnehmen!* (You must be crazy to go to Shanghai. You might as well take your coffin with you.)"

When Mutti first broached our possible emigration to Shanghai, Vati pooh-poohed the idea. Let us wait for the American visa. How long can it take? We are better off waiting here in civilized Breslau rather than in some godforsaken rathole. And so, we waited.

At the beginning of November 1938, Mutti decided to take a trip to the American Consulate in Berlin to investigate the status of our visa. She was also going to try to obtain a visitor's visa to England in case the American Consulate would issue us a visa via England.

While she was away, on November 7, in Paris, the Holocaust started.

Herschel Grynspan, an unstable seventeen-year-old Polish Jew, whose family was living as stateless refugees in Hanover, Germany, became very upset and depressed when they were deported. While in Paris, he purchased a pistol, entered the German Embassy and shot the Third Secretary, Ernst Vom Rath, who had been sent to inquire what he wanted. The Germans then announced that should Vom Rath die from his wounds, there would be heavy reprisals against the Jews of Germany.

Vom Rath did succumb from his wounds on the afternoon of November 9, and all hell broke loose.

Chapter 13

KRISTALLNACHT, NOVEMBER 9–10, 1938, the night of broken glass, will be remembered as the beginning of the end for European Jewry.

When the news came that Vom Rath was dead, Goebbel's propaganda machine went into action, whipping up the people to take revenge on innocent Jews. Throughout the night of November 9–10, widespread attacks were made on Jews and Jewish-owned property. Synagogues were burned, store windows were smashed, and Jewish males were arrested for the crime of being Jewish. The event went down in history as *Kristallnacht.*

No complete tally exists of the destruction, but at least 30,000 Jews were arrested (approximately 8,000 in Austria) and sent to concentration camps at Sachsenhausen, Buchenwald and Dachau. According to a report prepared by the infamous Reinard Heydrich himself, 815 shops were destroyed, and 29 warehouses and 171 dwellings set on fire or otherwise destroyed; 191 synagogues were torched and a further 76 completely demolished. Thirty-six Jews were killed and thirty-six severely injured. This was only a provisional report, however, prepared immediately after the event. Historical research has since indicated that the degree of destruction was much greater.

In addition, the government imposed a fine of one billion marks on the Jews, confiscated all insurance claims, and introduced decrees facilitating the intensified "aryanization" of German economic life. The fine and the profits accruing to the state from arynization, were intended to finance the German rearmament program, jeopardized at this time by the expiration of credits from the Reichsbank. The *Aktion*—along with suppression of the Jewish press and Jewish cultural and commercial organizations—may have been considered as a form of pressure on German and Austrian Jewry to emigrate, which did accelerate, once the arrested Jews were released early in 1939.

The November *Kristallnacht* marked a turning point in the treatment of German and Austrian Jewry. Thereafter, there was no place for them in the German economy, and no independent Jewish life was possible.

Chapter 14

On that fateful morning of November 10, 1938, I rose at the usual time, had breakfast, and waited for Ilse to walk me to school. Mutti was away in Berlin, and Vati was planning his day's work, supervising the paper cutting and the packing of some merchandise for shipping.

Ilse was a little late and I was jumping with impatience by the time she arrived, not wanting to be late for school. She was out of breath as if she had been running. "I don't think you will be going to school today," she panted.

"Why not?" I said surprised.

"*Ach, Herr Popielarz*," cried Ilse, as soon as Vati appeared. "*Es ist schrecklich was hier vorgeht* (it's terrible what is happening). Look out of the window. The sky is black, the smoke of all the burning synagogues."

We rushed to the windows. And indeed the sky was black with billows of smoke. But we heard no fire engines.

Vati rushed for the radio, but all we heard was martial music. "Don't move," he told us. He went out into the street to see what was going on, and then came back rather quickly, his face white.

"Ilse, you go home," he said. "Evelinchen, take a change of clothing and your night things, *you* are going over to the Kiewes'." Frau Kiewe was a good friend of the family, a divorcée living with her mother and a daughter, Ruth, who was five years older than I. They lived on Kronprinzenstrasse, only a few minutes' walk from our apartment.

"We will wait till Edith gets here so she can take care of Omi, and then we'll leave," Vati said.

Edith now worked for us only on a part-time basis. One day, very apologetically, she told us that her husband, who was a driver for a delivery firm, had had to join the Nazi Party or it would have cost him his job. "But we're no Nazis," she assured us.

Martha would still visit occasionally, even though she was very nervous and kept looking over her shoulder. Her visits even got Vati nervous so that as soon as she arrived, he would leave the house. This way, in case anyone spied her coming to see us, there would be no Jewish male in the same house and the charge of *Rassenschande* could not be leveled at him.

When Edith walked in, she was in tears. *"Herr Popielarz, gehen sie sofort weg. Suchen Sie einen Versteck. Man verhaftet alle Juden die man auf der Strasse sieht.* (Go off and hide, quickly, they are arresting Jews all over the place)."

Vati and I left immediately. Edith was going to stay with Omi till Mutti got back from Berlin. My father dropped me off quickly at the Kiewes' and told us he would go into hiding. Frau Kiewe said she would take good care of me.

Two days later Mutti returned from Berlin. Her trip had been fruitless. As soon as the first synagogue was put to the torch, the beginnings of *Kristallnacht*, the American Consulate had closed its doors. She never got to see anyone to check our papers. Edith told her where I was staying and she came to pick me up. "Where's Benno?" she inquired. We did not know.

She called up various friends, and then we found out that all the Jewish men had disappeared, and no one knew where they were. The authorities would not tell us either. So we waited.

A week after *Kristallnacht*, we received a postcard from Vati, postmarked "Buchenwald." Buchenwald? Where was that? We had never heard of the place.

"Ich sitze hier ein," he wrote. (the German word *"einsitzen"* means to serve a prison term. *"Sitze hier ein,"* literally has no meaning.)

"That's peculiar language," Mutti mused. "I wonder what he is trying to say?"

He asked her to send some warm clothing, which seemed logical, because he probably only wore his business suit, winter coat, and spats. He hadn't even taken gloves.

Quickly, Mutti packed a large box with warm underwear, woolen socks, sweaters, jackets and blankets, and shipped them off to this Buchenwald place. We found out that all our friends' wives received similar innocuous postcards with the same request for warm clothing.

I then heard Mutti speaking on the phone with Frau Kiewe, "I'm going to Hamburg," she said firmly, "to purchase steamship tickets for the first available ship to Shanghai. Why don't you come with us—you, your mother and Ruth?" But Frau Kiewe wouldn't leave. She felt her mother was too sick and too old to travel. Ruth was leaving for Palestine on a youth transport.

Next, Mutti telephoned Frau Gumpert, another close friend who had also received a card from her husband from Buchenwald with the same peculiar wording. Perhaps he and Vati were together. Frau Gumpert told Mutti she would go to Hamburg with her, and it was agreed that we would all leave for Shanghai together.

The first available ship for Shanghai was the *Hakozaki Maru*, a Japanese vessel leaving February 13, 1939 from Naples, Italy. Mutti immediately purchased three tickets, all she could afford. If Vati was released from Buchenwald in time, the three of us would leave for Shanghai, and we would arrange for Omi to follow as soon as we were set up for her. If he didn't get home in time, Omi would leave with us and he would follow.

From Hamburg, Mutti cabled Uncle Moritz in Manchester. Could he arrange for "board money" to be deposited with the Nippon Yusen Kaisha Line in Hamburg without which the steamship company would not give us our tickets to Shanghai? The money would be returned to him as soon as we were able.

A few days later, a cable from Manchester was delivered to the hotel: NECESSARY MONEY DEPOSITED WITH NIPPON YUSEN KAISHA LINE IN NAME OF RIKA POPIELARZ. She returned to Breslau with the three precious tickets in hand.

December 5 was Mutti's forty-seventh birthday, At five o'clock that morning, we were awakened by the ominous sound of the doorbell. Gestapo! we all thought. While Omi and I huddled in the hallway, Mutti opened the door a crack. We heard a scream and there was Vati—haggard, head shaven, but nevertheless our beloved Vati.

We hugged and kissed. We were all crying. It was so good to have him back again.

"Sie haben dir alle Locken abgeschnitten. (They cut off all your curls)," wailed Omi.

Then Vati told us what had happened.

After he had dropped me off at the Kiewes', he went to the office on Lothringerstrasse, planning to go into hiding. Herr Kogel, the landlord, met him in the courtyard. "Herr Popielarz," he cried, "you can't be out on the street right now! Don't you know they're arresting all Jews? Come into my apartment immediately, and my wife and I will put you up."

So Vati stayed with the Kogels, who generously hid him from the Nazis. When they listened to the radio the next morning, November 11, they heard Goebbels, Hitler's Propaganda Minister, announce that the raid was over, there would be no more arrests. Vati decided the coast was clear and, against the Kogels' better judgment, he left their home. He went straight to the Kiewes' apartment house to pick me up and rang the bell. As he waited for Frau Kiewe to open the door he rang again, and a moment later the Gestapo walked into the building.

"*Ausweis.*" Vati handed over his identification papers. "*Jude, Sie kommen mit uns.* (You are coming with us, Jew)."

He was taken to the local precinct, where numerous Jews were already waiting. Among them was his friend Herr Gumpert. They were not allowed to talk to each other. After a while some

Offices and warehouses of RIPO Paper and Twine, Breslau; also where my father had been hidden by the Christian landlord during *Kristallnacht.*

army trucks came, and they were told to get in. *"Einsteigen! Schnell!"*

They climbed up into these trucks and were told to sit and keep their heads down—they were not to look up or out. After about ten minutes the truck stopped. *"Alle aussteigen!"* Everyone got out of the truck, wondering what was going to happen to them now. What met their eyes was a sad sight. They were facing what had been one of the most beautiful showpieces in Germany, the *Neue Synagoge*.

This Reform synagogue, constructed during the 1880s, had been listed in all the German tourist literature as a must attraction. It was tremendous, had gilded rococo ornamentation, a choir box, and priceless crystal chandeliers. Even the Kaiser had been a guest at the synagogue during its inauguration. I had been a flower girl at a few weddings held there and remember its overpowering beauty. The Gestapo had tried to set it on fire, only it wouldn't burn, so they resorted to dynamite. The rabbi ran in and managed to save the Torahs, but the explosion blew off the cupola and left an enormous hole in the roof.

The Jewish prisoners were told to take a good look at the synagogue, and then they were loaded back onto the trucks. They traveled for many hours. Finally they reached their destination. A big sign greeted them: *BUCHENWALD*. They had only vaguely heard the name and surmised that it was one of the prisoner camps established by the Nazis for "political" prisoners. Now it was filled with Jews.

As the men were getting off the trucks, Vati noticed that many of them tripped or fell. Looking closer, he saw that some of the men were either pushed off the truck or deliberately tripped. He watched his step, and when the Nazi guard tried to trip them, Vati nimbly jumped over his foot.

The men were all settled into tiny bunk barracks. It was cold and damp, and they were not permitted to go to the latrine. They had no food or water for hours and only had the clothes that were on their backs. The next morning's breakfast consisted of a slice of black bread and some tepid water. There was no lunch. They were given striped prison uniforms, and had their heads shaved. For dinner, they were given whale meat to eat. By that time they were so hungry that they probably would have eaten a whole whale.

A few days later, when many of the men became ill, they realized that the meat must have been contaminated. They were then given a postcard to write home. They were told what to write ("now I know why the wording was so strange!" exclaimed Mutti) and to ask for warm clothing. Vati told us he never received the package from home, and neither did any of the other men. Obviously this was just another Nazi ruse to get some fine clothing from the Jews.

They were kept in constant suspense about what was going to happen to them. Some of the men had been beaten—for not standing up straight during roll call or speaking when not spoken to.

Then one day, the camp *Kommandant* made an announcement over the loudspeaker. Any veteran who had received the Iron Cross, First or Second Class, would be allowed to go home. Joyfully, hundreds of men, among them Vati, lined up in front. All veterans wore a little replica of the medal with a red, gold and black ribbon attached, on their lapels. The *Kommandant* was very taken aback when he saw how many Jews were veterans and had

This is the document that got my father out of Buchenwald early. It states that Benno Popielarz is in possession of the German Medal of Honor for his loyalty to the *Vaterland* during the World War. After it was reissued in pocket-size format in 1933, my father always carried it with him.

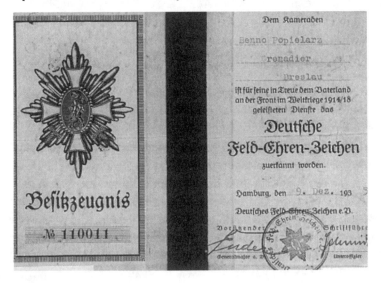

actually earned medals for valor. So he tried another ploy.

Of those in line, he wanted to know, how many had the original certificates with them—as proof that they had actually gotten their medals legitimately. Many faces fell. Only about one third of the veterans carried that precious paper on their persons. Vati had always kept it with him, in case he was ever challenged by the Gestapo. His foresight had now become his passage to freedom.

However, the *Kommandant* had one more card to play. Anyone who had either a cut or bruise on his person could not be released either. Vati, having made sure not to let himself get tripped, slipped out of this trap, too. Reluctantly, the Nazis let him and some other men go.

Once he was home, he had to sign in with the Gestapo every morning, promising that he and his family would be leaving Germany within two months.

Now it was Mutti's turn. With much trepidation, she told him how she had purchased three tickets for Shanghai and that we would have to leave Breslau on February 9, 1939. She watched Vati's face. How was he going to react? He wanted to go to America.

"Shanghai!" he exclaimed. "Good! Too bad we can't leave sooner. After Buchenwald, yesterday wouldn't be too soon to leave."

"Are you going to build some money into the typewriter platens to take out of Germany?" asked Mutti. It was an idea of hers for smuggling out more than the official allowance for living expenses.

"No, no," answered Vati. "After what I saw in Buchenwald, I would not take a chance on getting caught."

Now came the feverish arrangements for our departure. We had to have the passports validated, and make an exact list of all personal possessions we would be taking with us to Shanghai. Mutti decided to take salable items besides things we would need for everyday living, so that we would have some initial funds on arrival. She packed all our heavy linens, tablecloths, her furs, china, crystal, and all our silverplate flatware, among other things. When she was finished, she had fifty full pages itemizing all our possessions.

Vati, of course, took all of his suits, shirts, ties, and socks. He was always a very elegant and meticulous dresser. All his clothes were custom made. I remember the tailor coming over to measure him, and then the fittings with the white chalk marks. He had several shirts and other accessories to go with each suit, and he wore spats, highly fashionable in Germany at the time, to match each outfit. Luckily he had been wearing his spats when the Gestapo arrested him, for they helped keep his feet warm in Buchenwald.

Mutti had hoped that Buchenwald might have broken him of his smoking habit, for he had just recovered from a bout of nicotine poisoning. Before he was arrested, he had tried to stop and had bought himself a fake menthol cigarette, which he was able to smuggle into the camp. It did help keep his spirits up, but after his release, he went back to smoking, even more than before.

One morning, as Vati was standing on line for his daily sign-in at Gestapo Headquarters, the clerk whose line he was on chanced to look up as he gave him his identification. "Benno!" he exclaimed sheepishly, "*Wie geht es Dir?*" It was a former classmate of Vati's from the gymnasium.

The two old schoolmates greeted each other awkwardly. Then the clerk leaned forward. "From now on," he whispered, "just come over to me right away, and you won't have to stand in line to sign in." Vati was very grateful for this little courtesy. Now he would have more time to help Mutti with the travel arrangements.

More farewell get-togethers—one could hardly call them parties. Some of our friends were still waiting for visas and places to go, and some were also going to Shanghai. The Gumperts were traveling with us.

Mutti made arrangements with Edith to take care of Omi till we could send for her. At the same time we would also try to sponsor one of the salesmen, Herr Juliusburger, and his immediate family. They would accompany Omi on the long voyage.

Mutti contacted her brothers, Henoch in Frankfurt-am-Main and Samuel in Berlin. "Come with us to Shanghai," she begged. "No," they both replied. "We're rabbis, and Hitler won't harm us. And if he does, then it's G-d's will and there is nothing we can do about it."

"At least send your children," Mutti implored. But Herta, Samuel's daughter, then in her twenties and unmarried, refused to leave her parents. Henoch's twin sons did take our advice. Avrohom joined Moritz in England, where he was also subsequently interned on the Isle of Man and later shipped to an internment camp in Canada, where he spent the war years. (After the war, he joined the Lubavitch movement and directed a yeshiva in Montreal. I subsequently attended his son's wedding at Lubavitcher Headquarters in Brooklyn.) His brother Ruben joined Uncle Leo in Paris.

(Henoch and his wife were gassed in Auschwitz. Samuel, his wife and daughter were deported to the Littsmanstadt [Lodz] ghetto where they perished.)

Mutti and Vati wanted to inscribe some sayings into my autograph book before leaving Germany. I guess they felt that things were so uncertain they might never have the opportunity again. I recently looked at these inscriptions, and I thought my heart would break. Both inscriptions are dated January 4, 1939. Vati's reads as follows:

> *Schäme Dich nie ein Jude zu sein*
> *Gräme Dich nie ein Jude zu sein*
> *Stets sei Dein Glück, Dein Stolz, und Dein Ruhm*
> *Ein Kämpfer zu sein für's Judentum!*

> *Zum Andenken an Deinen Dich Liebenden*
> *Vati*

(Never be ashamed to be a Jew/Never be grieved that you are a Jew/Let it always be your fortune, your pride, and your glory/To be a fighter for Judaism!/In remembrance of your loving Vati)

Mutti Wrote:

> *Sei Deinen Eltern Lust und Freude.*
> *Mit Dank erkenne ihr Bemühn.*
> *Und nie tu' ihnen etwas zu Leide.*
> *Dann wird auf Dir ihr Segen blühn.*
> *Nur solchen Kindern geht es gut,*
> *Auf denen der Elternsegen ruht.*

Meinem lieben Evelinchen zur
Beherzigung von ihrer Mutter

(Be a joy and happiness to your parents./Appreciate all their efforts,/And never do anything to hurt them./Their blessings will then rest upon you./Only those children that have their parents' blessings will do well in life/To my dear Evelinchen with all my heart from her mother)

On February 2, 1939, just before our departure, Joseph made the following inscription, in the old German block letters:

Wenn du einst sitzt als Grossmama,
Im Lehnstuhl sitzt beim Grosspapa,
Und träumst von Deiner Jugend Glück
Dann denk einmal an mich zurück.

Zur Erinnerung von deinem dich liebenden
Joseph Boroschek

(One day when you are a grandma/And are sitting in a rocking chair with grandpa/And if you are dreaming of your youthful happiness/Then think a little bit of me./In remembrance of your loving Joseph Boroschek)

He was never to be heard from again.

Chapter 15

On February 8, 1939, Dr. Biberstein arrived at our apartment with his vaccination equipment, to inoculate us against various tropical diseases. Without the doctor's certificate, we would not receive the necessary exit visa. Under the doctor's signature there was a little stamp that Jewish physicians were required to affix onto any document. It bore the Star of David and read, *"Zur ärztlichen Behandlung ausschliesslich von Juden berechtigt,"* certifying that Dr. Biberstein was only entitled to treat Jews. The following morning, we boarded the train that was to take us to Italy and our ship to Shanghai. We were leaving Germany, the country of my birth, for good.

Of course, to me this was all very exciting. Being off school since *Kristallnacht*, and now traveling by train and then by ship on a long voyage, seemed like a great adventure. I had never been on a

This Police Certificate is basically a "good conduct" certification, and was valid strictly for emigration purposes for three months from date of issue, February 8, 1939. This document served as an "exit visa."

big ship before and could not imagine sleeping, eating and walking on it as if we were on land.

The mood on the train itself was tense and gloomy. It seemed to rattle along for hours and did not stop until late at night. We had crossed the Brenner Pass and had arrived at the German (actually Austrian)–Italian border. The Gestapo boarded the train to check the passengers' papers. Mutti admonished me to be very, very quiet.

They walked into our compartment. *"Heil Hitler. Papiere, Pass, Ausweis."* Everyone quietly produced the necessary papers, inwardly shaking and hoping that everything would be in order. The men checked and counted the pieces of luggage to see that they corresponded with the official lists we had submitted prior to our departure. They made sure that the gold wedding bands my parents were wearing and the gold watches that the three of us were wearing were the only valuables we were taking out with us.

Finally, they stamped our passports and got off the train, which was soon moving again. We had crossed the border and were now in Italy. Everyone broke out in smiles and started to cheer. Bottles of champagne seemed to appear from nowhere. The mood had changed.

We arrived in Naples in the morning and checked into a hotel near the pier. None of us felt very well, the aftermath of our vaccinations. I had a temperature as well as a swollen arm, where the injection site had been. No one was in a sightseeing mood, and we really didn't have any money to spare for shopping anyway. So we stayed in the hotel, had our meals, and got ready to board the *Hakozaki Maru*.

As we were walking up the ship's gangplank on the day of departure, Vati stopped, turned around, and said he'd be right back. "He's probably getting more cigarettes," mumbled Mutti under her breath. "Hurry up, the ship won't wait for you," she called after him.

"Don't worry, we have plenty of time," he replied.

Suddenly, a lady approached us. "You must be Moritz Nelken's sister," she exclaimed.

"Yes, I am," said Mutti, surprised. "But how could you know that?"

"Your hands. You have the same hands as your brother. My name is Frau Viktor, and this is my daughter Marion. I am a friend of your brother's from Berlin. He wrote me from England that you would be on this ship and to look you up. We are also going to Shanghai."

This was really a pleasant surprise—to meet a friend of Moritz'. We remained friends during all our years in Shanghai.

We were now being taken to our stateroom, which turned out to be a beautiful cabin. But we had no time to admire it. Vati had not appeared as yet, and we were getting very nervous. We went up on deck and looked out at the harbor of Naples with Mount Vesuvius in the distance. We heard the announcement requesting all visitors to leave, for the ship was ready to sail. Still no Vati.

The gangplank was pulled in, the anchor raised, the cables were released from their bollards, and we heard the ship's engine, Mutti was frantic. Where was Vati? The ship was moving away from the pier. A few minutes later the harbor pilot pulled up alongside the ship and a ladder was lowered to its deck. And a moment later, Vati clambered up the side.

Poor Mutti—limp with relief and also furious. How could he do this to her? He was almost left behind! I thought it was a great joke, and Vati thought so too.

Once the ship got underway, we started to familiarize ourselves with the facilities. We would be aboard for at least a month. It was breathtaking, the most luxurious surroundings. Nothing was lacking. There was a movie theater, swimming pool, sun decks, a gym, playroom for children and a beautiful dining room.

When we came down for dinner, we saw that a ship's officer had been assigned to each table. Dr. Watanabe, the ship's doctor, was seated at ours. He spoke some German and we became very fond of each other. I even had him write in my autograph book:

> T. Watanabe
> SS "Hakozaki Maru"
> I wish you prosperity and happiness and may
> God ever attend you!
> (Signed in Japanese characters)

Our first stop was Port Said, at the entrance to the Suez Canal. We were told that we would be stopping there for two days and would be allowed off to go sightseeing.

Port Said gave us our first taste of life in the Orient. Our arrival was greeted by a tumult of activity at the dock. Little boys beckoned us to throw money into the river so that they could dive and retrieve it. The city was crowded, noisy, and dirty, and we saw our first street beggars. We walked through the marketplace and purchased a few trinkets. Mutti bought me a little silver bangle bracelet, which is still in my possession.

Two of our passengers were a young honeymoon couple, and when we returned to the ship, they were among the missing. Rumor had it that they were going to make their way illegally into Palestine, which was only about 150 miles away. We never found out if they made it, but we'd like to think they did.

Now the ship weighed anchor and proceeded on its slow passage through the Suez Canal. At times it looked as if we would hit the sides of the canal as we inched our way through, following the Egyptian harbor pilot. Everyone was on deck watching. finally we were in the open sea again and on to our next port, Bombay, India.

The weather now started to warm up considerably, and we were able to shed our winter clothes. People forced smiles onto their faces and tried to pretend that they were on vacation. As I was lounging around the playroom one day, a Japanese lady approached me. She was on her way home to Tokyo after having spent some time in Berlin, and she spoke a little German. She asked me to correct her grammar, and we ended up as teacher and pupil.

In her very broken German, she would tell me fascinating stories about life in Japan, the beautiful flowers and the gentle people. I asked her to write something in my autograph book to remember her by. She wrote a full page in Japanese, which a ship's officer then transcribed into English:

> *Mein liebes Evelinchen* (wrote Mrs. Tatamatsu in German—followed by text in Japanese)
> You were a very lovely and clever little lady, and as my teacher of German, you gave me very good lessons.
> Please do not forget forever this chance by which

we have become acquainted on board, and whenever you read this, call me back in your mind. I trust in Japan we shall have the sun beautifully shining as ever, under which lovely flowers like you will bloom. When you have grown up, come and see me.

12.3. [March 12] 1939

Upon our arrival in Bombay, we were told that we could not get off the ship, for we would only be stopping for a few hours. However, we were allowed off at the next port of call, Colombo, the capital of Ceylon (now Sri Lanka), the big island southeast of India. We were to spend two days in port while the ship took on provisions, as well as passengers.

The weather was brutally hot, and we did not do too much walking around. However, we hired a rickshaw, our first experience with this Oriental taxi, which would become very familiar in the next eight years. At a Buddhist temple, we had to leave our shoes outside—Mutti wondered whether we'd ever get them back—where a huge, gilded Buddha sat on a throne, and people prostrated themselves before him and burned incense. The women wore beautifully colored silk saris, and many had red caste marks on their foreheads or a jewel inserted in their noses.

The mood of the Jewish passengers on the ship, all of them refugees from Germany and Austria, had been steadily rising from the moment the ship left Naples. The fact that we were now physically far from the European continent and the Nazis made everyone feel lighthearted.

Evenings, after dinner, entertainment would be provided by the ship's master of ceremonies, a dapper little Japanese who spoke German passably well and some English too. The refugees who made up the majority of the passengers on board, also provided their own entertainment. One evening someone would play the piano while everyone gathered around and sang old German and Viennese college songs and operatic melodies. Another time, Vati, as the "resident ventriloquist," became the impromptu emcee and ship's comedian.

Mutti and Mrs. Viktor then composed a song, *"Wir fahren auf der Hakozaki.* . . (We're traveling on the Hakozaki. . .") sung to the tune of a popular German melody.

The ship's playroom contained toys for almost every age group, from a rocking horse and blocks to a little piano and windup record player. My favorite room was the gym. I loved swinging from the parallel bars, climbing the ropes, and sitting on the automatic rocking horse. I still wasn't too thrilled about swimming, but loved the movies, mostly popular German ones, though some were Shirley Temple films dubbed in German. I had always thought that Shirley Temple was German, particularly after having seen her movie *Lockenköpfchen* (*Curly Top*). There were many other refugee children in my age group on board, so I never lacked for playmates.

Every morning, at eleven o'clock, while everyone was relaxing on deck in their lounge chairs, the waiters would come around with hot bouillon. In the afternoon, it would be tea. Vati had organized a card game that was popular in Germany, called Skat.

I think everyone realized that this would probably be the last moments, for a long time, when life would seem so carefree and luxurious. (Many of these refugees would not survive the years in Shanghai.)

After departing Colombo, the First Class passengers were advised not to go below deck for any reason. The new passengers who

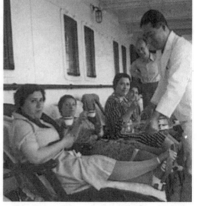

February 1939—on the *Hakozaki Maru* to Shanghai. Left photo: author is on the left. Right photo: mother second from right, being served 11 o'clock bouillon.

had boarded at Colombo, were settled on the outside lower deck where they ate and slept on mats. We had no idea why these Sinhalese were traveling to China. I remember looking down at the little children, who had no toys and looked hungry. Every day, after breakfast, I would throw down some bananas and rolls to them. They clambered over each other to get at the food. Never having lacked for food in my short life, I had no idea what it was to be hungry. I would soon find out.

At Singapore, we were allowed off the ship. We were now in the Far East. Everyone seemed to be wearing white and speaking English with a curious lilt, similar to the accent we heard in Ceylon. Vati, the linguist, had already picked up some English vocabulary and managed to make himself understood passably well.

Most of us could not understand what people were saying, they seemed to be very friendly. I had made a new friend, a young Malaysian, who had been studying in London and was returning home to Singapore. He and I would spend time in the gym or play dominoes. He was very curious about the refugees on the ship and tried to teach me some English. When we docked, he took the time to show us around the city, and I was sorry to part from him. He inserted the following poem, "The Highwayman's Legacy" written in 1751, into my autograph book:

> Beware of paper, pen, and ink;
> Beware of Talking when you drink;
> Beware of saying what you think;
> For many good fellows have swung in a noose
> For letting their tongues or their pens run loose.

It was many years before I understood the poem's message.

Our last important port of call was Hong Kong, a British Crown Colony on the Island of Victoria, and well known as a stopping place in the Orient. We were getting close to our destination. The ship had docked at night and it was really exciting to be out sightseeing in a strange city with Mutti and Vati when almost everyone was asleep. We got the impression of a bustling, Eastern metropolis, yet the British influence could be felt all around us. We wondered if Shanghai would be similar.

The following morning, the captain announced that we would be making a short, unscheduled stop at a little island (I don't remember the name) between Hong Kong and Shanghai, but we wouldn't be getting off. People began to get edgy. In two days we would be in Shanghai.

Right after we left the island, the heavens literally opened up—our first typhoon. The ship tossed back and forth on enormous waves that sometimes washed over the deck. Ropes were strung all over the ship for us to hold on to, yet people still slipped and fell. We were given strict instructions not to go out even on the upper deck, and to don life jackets.

My heart went out to the poor passengers on the open lower deck. They had lashed themselves together so they wouldn't be washed overboard and of course, being closer to the level of the sea, they were repeatedly drenched. But there was nothing we could do for them.

In First Class movies were shown, so that those few passengers who could still walk around would have something to do. Most of the passengers were seasick, including Mutti. Vati and I were among the few who were not.

I heard people praying. "What are they praying for?" I asked Vati. At first he didn't reply, and I thought he hadn't heard my question, so I repeated it.

Finally, after giving it some thought, he replied—reluctantly it seemed to me—"They are praying for the ship to sink."

I couldn't believe it. After traveling so far, to what seemed to me an exciting new place, why should people want to drown? "But why, Vati?"

"They are frightened about what they will find in Shanghai."

That was puzzling. "Are you frightened too? Do you want the ship to sink?"

"Oh, no," Vati replied, "we'll be starting a new life there, and I intend to live a long time yet, *liebes Evelinchen.*" Then I knew everything was going to be all right. My Vati could not be wrong about something like this.

The next day, the monsoon winds died down, and it stopped raining. Everything was back to normal, and we were packing again.

It was our last night on the *Hakozaki Maru*. The ship's officers had arranged a banquet, and everyone wore his or her best clothes. The dinner was magnificent, and all the children were allowed to stay up with the adults and share in the festivities.

I still remember the band playing all the familiar German melodies that I had heard on the radio and on our gramophone at home in Breslau. My parents joined in the singing. The mood was very gay. It must have been a false gaiety, because everyone was still apprehensive.

Germany was left behind, yet one could not forget relatives who were still there. Omi and Joseph, my uncles and cousins. Would they be able to follow us to Shanghai? Would they be safe in Germany till then? We wondered if we would ever return to the *Vaterland*. We had once loved it so much, and so many Jews had fought for it and died for it. And now. . . ?

Would this be the last time for dances, frivolity, good food, music, and dancing? Who knew? Let's make the best of it, was the attitude that prevailed on that last shipboard night.

The date was March 13, 1939. Tomorrow we would be starting a new life in a strange city, in an unfamiliar country with an unfamiliar language, climate, and people, where we would be safe and free.

PART II

A New Life
1939–1943

Typical Shanghai street scene during monsoon season.

Prologue to Part II: Shanghai

The city rose out of a mudbank about five hundred years ago. It lies on the banks of the Whangpoo River which empties into the Yangtze River, in the province of Kiangsu. In 1939, it had a population of approximately four million Chinese and 100,000 foreigners, a mixture of every country, particularly Americans, British, French, Germans, Russians, Japanese, Indians, plus the inevitable Eurasians, products of this very racially mixed society.

There were also two firmly entrenched Jewish communities. The older one consisted of Sephardim (Bagdhadi), and the larger was composed of Ashkenazim hailing mainly from Russia who had fled the 1917 revolution.

The Americans, numbering approximately 3,000, were mainly business people, administering branch offices of United States companies active in Asia.

The British, numbering approximately 11,000, were more firmly entrenched, Britain still being a colonial power at that time. Besides the business interests, they administered the International Foreign Settlement, commonly known as the Settlement, a sector of Shanghai housing the government facilities, hotels, air-conditioned office buildings, fine stores, the YMCA with its Olympic size swimming pool, and schools. The sector started at the Bund, Shanghai's famous waterfront district. Here were the large, international banks, the Customs House and warehouses, and Nanking Road was its main thoroughfare, considered the Fifth Avenue of Shanghai.

All sporting events were held at the Race Course which was located on Nanking Road.

To the south was the Concession Française, the residential section, which was administered by the French, who numbered approximately 2,500. Fine shops, beautiful apartment houses, parks and villas were situated along the beautiful, tree-lined streets. Most of the residents in this sector were Caucasian. The main avenue was the broad, impressive Avenue Joffre, named after one of France's World War I commanders in chief. A tramway ran the entire length of the avenue, stopping just before Nantao, the Chinese city.

To the north of the Settlement was the Garden Bridge, separating The Bund and the International Settlement from the sectors of Chapei, Hongkew, and the suburb of Yangtzepoo.

Japan had opened hostilities with China—large, poor, and torn apart by factions—in 1932 by occupying Manchuria (now the provinces of Heilongjiang, Jilin, and Liaoning), in the process of wiping out some 250,000 guerilla resisters. In retaliation, the Chinese tried to boycott Japanese goods, for which crime the Japanese landed troops at Shanghai and began a steady encroachment on Chinese territory, often accompanied by atrocities. In 1937, full-scale war broke out. Shanghai was savagely bombed, the infamous rape of Nanking (Nanjing) appalled the world—even the Germans protested—and in 1938, the Japanese emerged victorious.

Even though the Japanese occupied Shanghai, the Settlement and French Concession were still administered by the British and French respectively. Only Hongkew was administered by the Japanese, who numbered approximately 20,000, and were now the real power in Shanghai.

During our early years in Shanghai, the occupation troops kept a low profile, and except for the ravages of Japanese bombings, most visible in the Hongkew section, we saw little of the war. We had problems of our own.

Shanghai had a sub-tropical climate. It was not unusual for the thermometer to register 140 degrees in the shade during the summer months. The macadam would be so soft that shoes would sink in and get stuck. Head covering had to be worn at all times, and whenever possible, one avoided being outdoors between noon and two o'clock in the afternoon. The winters were cold and harsh—no snow, but the monsoons brought a lot of rain. This, plus Shanghai's low-lying sea level, made for constant flooding during the monsoons. The sewage system was extremely poor. Dig five feet, and water would come up.

Every disease known to mankind ran rampant. The local population had some immunity to many of the diseases, but Caucasians, particularly western Europeans, did not fare as well. Inoculations were required three times a year to combat typhoid, paratyphoid, and cholera, but ensured only partial immunity. Malaria, transmitted by the mosquito, was also prevalent, manifesting itself in extreme cases of dysentery. Only smallpox could be successfully avoided by means of annual vaccinations.

All water, fruit, and vegetables had to be boiled at least five minutes past boiling point, and non-boilable fruit, such as oranges, tangerines, apples and bananas, had to be placed in a disinfectant for an hour before being peeled and eaten.

The Japanese residents always wore surgical masks outdoors, for they believed that it offered them some kind of protection from germs. Newly arrived immigrants were admonished to relinquish the European habit of handshaking to prevent personal contamination.

Much of the pollution was aggravated by the peasants' use of human excrement as fertilizer for their crops, and by the casual habits of the sampan population residing on the Whangpoo. Whole families made their homes on these little wooden boats, where they would eat, sleep, and wash, while it rocked to and fro in the murky water. All garbage and sewage was dumped overboard into the river. Little children would be raised on these sampans, and upon reaching adulthood, if they were lucky, they would have their own sampan to continue the cycle.

Chapter 16

On Tuesday, March 14, 1939, we got our first glimpse of the city that was to be our new home. It was a crisp, sunny day, and we were all hanging from the railing, curious as to what would be awaiting us.

I saw little Chinese boys scurrying back and forth among a multitude of people dockside, chattering away in a very strange tongue. All of a sudden, there was a commotion on one end of the pier. I saw a rickshaw pull up with an Englishman aboard. (Mutti knew he was English, because he wore a topi, and carried a swagger stick under his arm.) An argument with the coolie ensued, and then I saw an unbelievable sight. The man actually hit the coolie with his swagger stick. The coolie ducked under his rickshaw, then picked up the shafts and left in a hurry. Mutti muttered that there was probably a dispute over the fare. I would see similar occurrences in the future.

It was time to disembark. At the bottom of the gangplank, we were pleasantly surprised to be greeted by a cousin of Vati's—Herbert Haase, his wife Edith, and their little son Billie. They had left Breslau just before *Kristallnacht,* and we had been in touch with them. They had been informed by the American Consulate that they would be getting their visas to the United States within the next few months.

So that Mutti and I would not have to be put up in dormitories till we could find a place of our own, they graciously offered to make room for us in their tiny furnished apartment. Only Vati needed to stay in the dormitory.

We had to go through customs. Like everyone else, we had a lot of luggage—suitcases, as well as fully packed steamer trunks. The agents checked our papers and then proceeded to look through our luggage. Everything went smoothly till they got to Vati's trunk. Their eyes almost popped out! In that trunk were about fifty shirts, most of them silk, about one hundred ties, and as many pairs of socks of various colors and lengths, shoes, pajamas, underwear, summer coats, winter coats with velvet collar and fur collar, and approximately forty custom-made wool suits all with their matching vests, as well as a dozen pairs of spats.

"Are you going into the clothing business, Herr Popielarz?" inquired the astonished official.

"Clothing business," sputtered Vati, deeply offended. "These are my *personal* suits, custom-made for me by my own tailor in Germany, and I intend to wear every one of them!"

The official shrugged his shoulders, probably thinking, "Crazy man! Wool suits in a tropical climate!" He would have laughed had he been present a few weeks later when Vati, having come to agree with him about the climate, ordered a dozen seersucker, sharkskin, and white linen suits made up, as well as some shorts sets.

We were next approached by the welcoming committee that had come to meet the refugee ships. This committee was made up of earlier arriving refugees plus social workers from the Joint (American Joint Distributing Committee), who had come from the United States to assist in resettling the refugees. Besides the funds from the Joint, there was also a British Fund that had been established by the Sephardic philanthropist, Sir Victor Sassoon who also owned the Embankment House. This building also served as a temporary shelter for the incoming refugees—it was where Vati stayed. It actually had been a luxury office building, which even included a swimming pool.

After Vati was established in the Embankment House, Mutti and I went off with the Haases. Their one-bedroom apartment in the French Concession was not too far from the Settlement. They had Billie share their bed, while Mutti slept on the living room sofa, and I scrunched up in Billie's crib. Even though we were all very cramped, at least we were not in a dormitory with hundreds of strange people.

We scanned the newspapers every day looking for an apartment of our own and finally found a large furnished room on the Rue Cardinal Mercier, in the French Concession, which would be our temporary shelter till we could get something more suitable. At least we would not have to disrupt the Haases any longer, and the refugees at the Embankment were delighted to get rid of Vati, for he kept everyone up with his snoring. (Vati claimed he couldn't understand what was bothering them; he had slept very well and never heard a thing!)

Mutti and I left the Haases' tight quarters (they must have been happy to see us go though they never said it), and moved at the end of

March. They received their visa for the United States a few months later, and were off to Chicago, where Edith had some relatives. We saw them embark, hoping we would soon be able to follow them.

My parents now had two important items on their agenda. Vati had to go out to earn a living, and I had to go back to school. We needed money to live on, and I had not seen the inside of a classroom for the last five months. Mutti also followed her preconceived plan of selling some of her personal possessions: her fox stole, and her Persian lamb coat, some of the fine linens, and bone china, allowing them to open a bank account.

When the established Sephardi community realized how many of the German and Austrian refugees had brought personal luxury items to sell, they set up the Thrift Shop. This stabilized the selling process and enabled the refugees to obtain reasonable prices for their valuable possessions.

Vati found a small office and workplace at 679 Szechuen Road in the Settlement. He quickly installed a telephone, had business cards and stationery printed, and hung up his shingle, "RIPO TYPEWRITERS." He then hired Yih Ah Kung, who was an experienced typewriter mechanic.

Both parents made the rounds of the various international firms in the Settlement to solicit customers. Mutti went after the German-speaking firms, and Vati, being fluent in French, concentrated on French-speaking customers, as well as American and British firms, having already improved upon his scant knowledge of English.

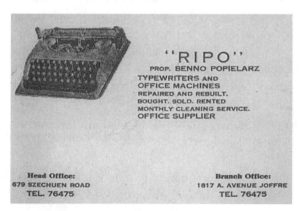

"RIPO"
PROP. BENNO POPIELARZ
TYPEWRITERS and
OFFICE MACHINES
REPAIRED AND REBUILT.
BOUGHT. SOLD. RENTED
MONTHLY CLEANING SERVICE.
OFFICE SUPPLIER

Head Office:
679 SZECHUEN ROAD
TEL. 76475

Branch Office:
1817 A. AVENUE JOFFRE
TEL. 76475

Father's Shanghai business card.

The business flourished almost immediately. Vati and Yih Ah did the servicing and repairs, how thankful we were that he had taken that mechanic's course back in Breslau, and Mutti took charge of the bookkeeping, correspondence and appointments.

Mutti had brought her bulky adding machine all the way from Germany. However, she soon became fascinated with the speed with which the Chinese did calculations on the abacus and persuaded Yih Ah to teach her how to use it. She never managed to attain speed, but she did so well with it that she finally gave up her old-fashioned adding machine.

Chapter 17

A decision as to which school I was to be enrolled in now had to be made. The choices were the French Aurora school, the British, Public Thomas Hanbury school (PTH), and the Shanghai Jewish School.

I was enrolled in the Shanghai Jewish School (SJS) at 544 Seymour Road in the Settlement. This school had been founded and was being subsidized by the wealthy and philanthropic Sephardi families, the Kadoories and Sassoons. It was a beautiful, greystone two-story, corner structure, with a large playground and hockey field, enclosed by a high wrought-iron fence with two enormous gates. These were always kept locked during school hours, but a small door within each gate allowed passage. There was also an imposing Sephardic synagogue at the far end of the school grounds.

The grades were Kindergarten through Form VI Upper, which was the graduating class. It was modeled after the British school system, with the curriculum made up in Cambridge, England. Test papers were sent to Cambridge for marking and returned to Shanghai fully graded. English was the teaching language, second language French. Hebrew and religion were combined as one class, with emphasis on prayer and, to a lesser degree, grammar and vocabulary. However, even though Hebrew was taught with the Sephardic pronunciation, which is the same as *Ivrit*, the Hebrew spoken in Israel, this education followed the prevailing mode, lacking in conversational Hebrew.

The faculty was composed of British, Dutch and British-trained Russian teachers. Tiffin (lunch), which was of course kosher, was included in the tuition. If a student was unable to pay the full tuition, the fee was reduced. When necessary, the student was fully subsidized by the school.

The school administration was faced with the dilemma of overenrollment. Numerous refugee children of school age had been arriving since mid-1938 and in increasing numbers by 1939. These children were Jewish and wanted to attend the only existing Jewish school in Shanghai. Another Jewish school was needed. Sir Horace Kadoorie, under the auspices of the Shanghai Jewish Youth Association, was instrumental in arranging the purchase of a tract of land in Hongkew where a school was established under the name of SYJA, though always commonly referred to as the Kadoorie School. It was staffed mainly with refugee teachers. The Hongkew district was picked because the majority of the refugees had settled there. Housing was cheap and many of the *Heime*, the dormitory-like buildings, for those refugees who did not have the means to locate elsewhere, were maintained in Hongkew, as were the soup kitchens built with Joint funds. Laura Margolies, one of the American staff members of the Joint had taken this project in hand.

I still remember the day my parents enrolled me in the Shanghai Jewish School. It was a bleak, rainy day in April, just before Passover. We had just participated in our own personal exodus, and the timing seemed appropriate. We hailed a double rickshaw, and I sat on Vati's lap.

We had to climb up a long flight of steps to reach the lobby of the school building, with its marble floor and huge windows, and carved trophy case. We were immediately ushered into the headmaster's office where Vati spoke to him in halting English. When Vati discovered that the headmaster spoke French, the conversation switched to that language and went much smoother.

The headmaster summoned a student from one of the upper classes to show me around the school. She was also a German refugee who had been in the school since the end of 1938, so I had no communication problems.

Everything was quite impressive and very different from the Wohlschule in Breslau. The classrooms were spacious, with many windows and comfortable-looking desks. I would be assigned a desk with its own fountain pen and nibs. The gym, which doubled as an assembly room, contained the Union Jack and a lifesize portrait of King George VI and Queen Elizabeth. There was a library, chemistry laboratory, and a small infirmary. I wondered how I was going to understand the teachers who, of course, taught in English. I was soon to find out.

While I was gone, my parents had filled out all the necessary forms and paid the tuition for the balance of the school term, which was to end in June. They also informed me that I would now be using the original name they had picked for me at the time of my birth: Evelyn Popielarz. Of course, now that we were out of Germany, Mutti and I could both drop our Nazi-given middle name of Sara, and Vati could drop the Israel.

When the headmaster escorted me to my classroom, I was quite upset that it was not the one I had just been in. Not only that, but I was put into Kindergarten.

I was eight-and-a-half years old, and I had had over three years of schooling. It was a shock finding myself in baby class. But I was not alone in this predicament. There were other refugee children in the class, and we were told that we would be in Kindergarten only for a very short time just enough to learn rudimentary English.

The school administration, we learned later, had decided on a very simple and efficient way of dealing with refugee students who spoke no English, mostly German, but also some of the Slavic tongues. Language, the administration felt, is absorbed easiest at its most elementary level. If the children learned their first words of English in Kindergarten, it would enable them to catch up in a short span of time, and soon function at their proper level.

Mrs. Hekking, a rather severe looking blond lady, was the teacher. She explained to me in halting German that she was Dutch and that many Dutch people spoke some German, for the languages were similar. The first day of class we were making cutouts from coloring books that were going to be pasted on a board. I was looking for the scissors. I approached the teacher:

"*Kann ich bitte eine Schere haben?*"

Mrs. Hekking brought me a pair of scissors. Before handing them to me, she said, "these are scissors. Repeat after me: *scissors.*"

I repeated, "*tseezerrs.*"

"Now say, 'Please give me a pair of scissors'."

"Plees giff me a pehrr off tseezerrs."

"*Das war sehr gut,* very good," complimented Mrs. Hekking.

The following day I had to ask for some colored pencils. "*Bitte,* plees, *kann ich die Farbstifte haben?* Giff me."

Patiently, Mrs. Hekking had me translate the sentence into

English. And so it went. Anytime I had to ask for something, part of the sentence, at least, had to be in English.

Every morning we had assembly in the gym. The Union Jack was raised, and we all sang "God Save the King," followed by "*Hatik-vah.*" So now I had to learn a new anthem. Not only did I never again have to sing "*Deutschland, Deutschland, Über Alles,*" but we were told that no German was to be spoken in school—ever. Anyone caught speaking German had to pay a small fine.

School discipline was adhered to very strictly, also patterned after the British school system. Students caught speaking out of turn, or to another student during class, were made to stand outside the classroom door. This in itself wasn't so bad, but there was always the fear that the headmaster might walk by. If he saw a student standing in the hall, he would ask what the punishment was for, and then the student would be admonished by him. If he saw the same student too often, or if the teacher reported that the student was misbehaving more than usual, then it meant being sent down to the headmaster and having to stand in front of the trophy case in the lobby. Any student caught speaking to another student under punishment would also get punished, in a similar fashion. Once sent to the headmaster, the punishment would often be a caning on the palm of the hand with a ruler.

When the teacher walked into the classroom in the morning, we all had to rise and chant, "Good morning, Mr. . . ." or "Good morning, Mrs. . . ." If another teacher or the headmaster walked in while class was in session, we also had to rise. Anyone not rising would get reprimanded.

There was also a dress code. White blouse and navy tunic for the girls and white shirt and blue shorts—or long pants, depending on the season—for the boys. (It was called a tunic, but was actually a jumper in the American sense.)

School was going to be over the end of June, and preparations were underway for the big yearly sports event at the Shanghai Race Course. All the children in every grade school in the city were to participate. One Sunday morning in June, we all assembled for the big event. I really had no idea what was happening. I was told to stand in line with about ten other children and that, at the command "ready, set, go," I was to run. So I did. The next thing I knew, I was way ahead of all the other children and had reached a ribbon strung across the track. I was handed a blue ribbon with a big gold Number 1 on it and a beautiful doll.

I subsequently ran the three-legged race, where I practically dragged my slower partner along the track, and then I participated in the sack race. Not only did I get the most ribbons of anyone I knew that day— and the doll—I got my name into the *North China Daily News.*

My parents were thrilled, especially Vati. "Can you imagine," he trilled to anyone who would listen, "here we are, refugees from Germany, in Shanghai but a few weeks, and already Evelinchen has gotten her name into the newspapers."

Chapter 18

My parents were now very impatient to move into their own apartment. They were doing well financially in their typewriter business, and the furnished room we were in was much too small for us to unpack our suitcases and trunks, most of which were still in storage. It was also vermin infested.

Actually, for the Orient, that was not unusual. The most hazardous pests were the lice and mosquitos. The lice carried typhus and the mosquitos malaria. Every hour on the hour we would spray the premises with Flit and only sleep under mosquito netting. There was not much we could do about the other bugs.

We became quickly familiar with large red centipedes that would crawl up the wall and then proceed to lunch on whatever was in sight. Their bite would raise a painful welt on the skin, which would take days to disappear. The bites of the fat red spiders, also in abundance, had about the same effect. The most annoying were the flying cockroaches, about the size of a large beetle. Though repulsive, they were comparatively harmless. They would shamelessly sit about almost anywhere and then fly away very quickly before we had a chance either to swat them or spray them. Their rectangular eggs, about two centimeters in size, with little teeth at the edge, would attach themselves to clothing, usually in drawers, where it was dark and damp. Everything in Shanghai was damp, and things became mildewed very rapidly. Mutti had brought a lot of *Seidenpapier* (tissue paper) with her from her business, as well as an enormous amount of wrapping paper, twine, and blotting paper. She would thus wrap most of our articles of clothing to keep the mildew from spreading. Yet, even with all these precautions, a damp odor emanated from all our drawers.

Over the years we lived in Shanghai, I learned to brace myself anytime I opened a cupboard or drawer, warily watching for cockroaches, and then I would carefully examine the clothing for eggs before dressing myself.

The rats were much more dangerous, for they scurried about during the night and would attack almost anything. Of course we laid traps, but that helped only somewhat. When Mutti was nearly attacked by an aggressive rat, that was the last straw. "We're moving immediately," she declared. "In our own apartment we would have a little control over vermin."

Adjustment to everyday life in the Orient was not easy for us. In Germany the streets were immaculate—no one would even dare to discard even the smallest piece of paper—whereas Shanghai was absolutely filthy. Garbage was strewn about almost everywhere we looked. Urinating in public against a wall was a common sight. The Chinese did not believe in using handkerchiefs either, considering them unsanitary and the spreader of germs, so when they sneezed, it was into their hands, which they would wipe off on the nearest public surface.

No matter where we went, we would be besieged by beggars or followed by little children pulling at us or banging at the side of the rickshaw with their plaintive cry: "No mama, no papa, no whiskey, no soda," which we understood to mean that they lived in the streets and were begging for food.

We wanted to live in the French Concession, away from the hubbub and the slumlike buildings in Hongkew. Mutti was struck by a particular advertisement in the paper, and after school, she and I took the tram to the end of Avenue Joffre. From there we walked down a tree-lined lane, passing various small villas.

At the end of this lane we approached a red wrought-iron gate, and the watchman directed us to Mr. Lifschitz, the landlord. We rang the bell, and a moment later, a stocky man, with horn-rimmed glasses, opened the door and looked us over.

"Mr. Lifschitz" Mutti said politely.

"Yes, what can I do for you?"

Mutti pointed to the ad in the newspaper and said, in her halting English, "apartment for rent here."

"*Sprecht ihr Yiddish?*" was the reply.

Mutti perked up happily, "*Ja, ja, ich sprech Yiddish,*" she replied in her German-accented Yiddish. Now she could converse in a tongue they both understood.

This was only the second time in my life that I heard Yiddish spoken and I could not understand one word, for German Jews, as a rule, did not speak Yiddish. However, Mutti was very familiar with that language because Omama Miriam had spoken it.

Mr. Lifschitz told Mutti that he had only one apartment vacant, and his agent had told him that someone had seen it and would give him an answer in a day or two. Mutti persuaded him to show it to us anyway.

We liked it immediately, and I was hoping we could move in right away. The apartment had two outside entrances—one from the front and one through the kitchen. It was situated on the ground floor at the corner of one of the buildings, which contained different size apartments, all with their own outside entrances.

There were two small bedrooms on the right side of the corridor, next to a small bathroom. On the left was the living room and a small bedroom. Beyond that was a large kitchen and a large bathroom. There were lots of windows which made it look very cheerful.

After we had seen the apartment, Mutti and Mr. Lifschitz went into a deep discussion in Yiddish mixed with German. Here and there I could pick out a familiar word when it sounded like German. Was he going to rent to us or not? When I finally asked Mutti what they had discussed so much, she just said, "I'll tell you later when we get home to Vati."

Mr. Lifschitz then introduced to us to other refugee families, who had already moved into his compound, as housing and apartment groupings were called. The Ackermans and their twin daughters; the Fischers, and their daughters, who had escaped from Vienna right after the *Anschluss*; from our hometown, Breslau, there were the Weisses and their daughter; and the Rings and their daughter; Dr. and Mrs. Salomon, and their daughters from Berlin. All the other apartments were rented to Russians, mostly White Russians, we were told. I said to myself, he wouldn't be introducing us to everyone if he wasn't going to rent the apartment to us. So I felt very optimistic.

We went back to the Lifschitz apartment for tea and to meet his wife Julia and his young son, Zyama. Zyama invited me out to play and then proceeded to show me around the premises. First there was a garden with a summer-house, a kind of gazebo, and in the middle of the compound, around which all the buildings were constructed, there was a tremendous concrete planter with small flowers and bushes in the center.

When we got home, Mutti told Vati about Mr. Lifschitz . He had left his native Russia as a teenager, at the time of the 1917 Bolshevik Revolution, and had made his way, penniless, via Harbin and Vladivostok, to Shanghai. After some odd jobs, he managed to save a little money, enough to buy himself a small apartment. He then married Julia, who had a Soviet passport and had some money from a small inheritance. He started buying real estate, and the compound was his latest purchase. He wanted to thank God for having been so good to him, so he was going to build a little synagogue on the grounds where daily services would be held. Whereas his wife was pretty well educated, he was not. He could read Yiddish and some Russian, and even though he could speak English well, he was barely literate in the language.

"But did you get the apartment?" inquired Vati.

"Yes!" Mutti cried triumphantly. "You won't believe this, but the only reason Mr. Lifschitz decided to give me the apartment on the

spot—without waiting for the party to get back to him—was the fact that I, as a *Yäcke*, spoke Yiddish."

"*Yäcke*?" I echoed, "What's a *Yäcke*?"

Mutti explained to me that *Yäcke* is a pejorative term for German Jews, mostly used by Eastern European Jews.

My parents ordered furniture consisting of single-unit cupboards containing drawers, shelves, and hanging rods, which could be placed next to one another to give the impression of one unit,

Author with parents in garden at 1817 Avenue Joffre, Shanghai 1940.

or they could be moved to different parts of the apartment as needed.

We bought beds, a couch, living-room chairs, bridge table, a small unpretentious dining room set, as well as small area rugs, lamps, and curtains. Still adhering to European custom, we did not eat in the kitchen.

At the end of June, right after school was over, we moved to 1817A Avenue Joffre. Then began the big job of unpacking all the possessions we had brought from Germany. We had a telephone installed, which also served as an extension of the business phone, with the same telephone number, 76475.

Because both of my parents were involved in the business, we needed someone to take care of the apartment. We hired a Number One Boy and an amah. She had had her feet bound as an infant, for that had been the Chinese custom for females born before the October 1912 revolution. Small feet were supposed to be very pretty for females, and it was an indication of wealth and aristocracy, proving that they did not have to walk but would be carried by coolies in special chairs. Many peasant females also followed this custom, although it made life a little more difficult for these women who would then have to hobble in their little silk shoes. Sun Yat-Sen, who became president after the revolution, outlawed this archaic custom, together with the queue for Chinese males, but the binding of feet was still practiced in many households in the 1920s.

Mah Ling, our amah, had straightened out her crippled feet when she was about ten years old. She still hobbled a bit but walked better than others who never went through the straightening-out process. She also believed in rubbing the inside of each arm with the side of a spoon till it bled, as a cure for headaches, stomachache, a cold, or fever.

Mutti had the task of explaining to Mah Ling and Boy the rudiments of European—and kosher—cooking and to take all the precautionary hygienic steps to ensure that everything was boiled and properly cleaned before serving. Boy was given the additional task of being the *Shabbos goy*—that is, he was in charge of shutting off all the lights on the Sabbath when it was time to go to sleep.

Both Boy and Mah Ling spoke pidjin English, a mixture of Chinese and English. Considering that we barely spoke English, communication became even more complicated.

Chapter 19

In the meantime, we had registered with the American Consulate in Shanghai hoping to get our visa for the United States. However, we were still told that we had a very high number, and there would be a wait. How long? They could not tell us.

We realized that we would have to make the best of the situation and live as normal a life as possible till our departure for the United States. And who knew how long that would take?

In 1933, Russian Jews in Shanghai had formed a separate Jewish Company within the Shanghai Volunteer Corps (SVC). This was a part-time military group drawn from many of the nationals residing in Shanghai, including White Russian ex-soldiers. Vati was one of a handful of German refugees to join up with the SVC Jewish Company.

He proudly arrived home in his dress uniform and military equipment, which consisted of full battle dress, including boots and a helmet, as well as a pistol and rifle. While Mutti was aghast at this military display, I enjoyed watching him parade down The Bund, and going for battle training and target practice every Thursday. The rifle, which he taught me to handle, was always stored behind the living room

Father—contrasts in uniform. Left: as a German soldier in 1917. Right: as a member of the Jewish Company of the Shanghai Volunteer Corps in 1939.

door. Vati was always careful with it and made sure it was stored unloaded. Even though I handled the gun often, I never enjoyed it.

One day, when I came home from school, I was greeted by a little black furry puppy. Vati had just brought him home and named him Tasso. Mutti was not too happy with this addition to our family; he had to be trained, he shed all over the place, he had fleas. But I loved him. I had never owned a pet, and he was adorable. But Tasso was Vati's dog. He would not leave Vati's side, even slept at the foot of the bed right under his feet.

Vati's health had started to worry Mutti. Almost from the time we arrived in Shanghai, his old army wound started acting up. He thought that the queasy stomach was from his treatment in Buchenwald, and the rotten whale meat, compounded by the change in climate, and that in time he would feel better. Dr. Salomon, who was now our family doctor, could not find anything particularly wrong with him, but did suggest rest and extra precautionary measures with the food, and since Vati was continually running a low-grade fever, referred him to a tropical disease specialist. The specialist thought that the fever was caused by an infection that had settled in his gums, so Vati had most of his teeth pulled. The fever abated, and he started feeling a little better.

He then contracted jaundice, which was also not an unusual disease in Shanghai. He stayed in bed a couple of weeks and adhered to a very strict, greaseless diet, but he continued to smoke, even though he was advised to give it up.

What compounded Mutti's concern was the high attrition rate among the refugees. Most vulnerable were the elderly, infants, and those with a low resistance, many the survivors of the *Kristallnacht* concentration camp experience. The refugee community was particularly shaken by the recent death of a new arrival from Berlin, Rabbi Stein, a twenty-eight-year-old Buchenwald survivor. He had contracted typhus and died within a few days, leaving a young, grieving widow. They had gotten married just before leaving Germany.

The German refugee community had already formed their own Chevra Kaddisha, Jewish burial society, which purchased land on Columbia Road to be used as a Jewish cemetery. It started to fill up very quickly. A second refugee cemetery was planned on Point Road in Hongkew.

My grandmother's advice to the Gestapo of her emigration to Shanghai on the *Conte Verde* May 10, 1940, accompanied by Erich Israel Juliusburger.

Chapter 20

My parents set themselves to the task of getting all our relatives out of Europe. Immediately upon our arrival, they filed an application with the Shanghai office of the German Consulate to get Omi out, as well as Herr Juliusburger and his family. She also tried to sponsor another one of her salesmen and his family, the Klingbeils. However, they had already arranged passage on the ill-fated *St. Louis*—the ship that was turned back to Germany from Cuba.

Even though the applications were filed in June of 1939, getting German approval and steamship space took many months, for Jews were now leaving Nazi-occupied Europe by the thousands. Omi and the Juliusburgers were finally able to book passage on the SS *Conte Verde* of the Italian Lloyd Triestino line, leaving Genoa May 19, 1940.

(This was to be the ship's last voyage to Shanghai. When the

Mediterranean was closed by Italy's entry into the war in June, the only way of reaching Shanghai from Europe was by way of Russia and Siberia.)

After Hitler's invasion of Poland September 1, 1939, all correspondence with our Polish relatives ceased. However, Mutti was still corresponding with her German siblings trying to persuade them to leave. She thought that the deteriorating conditions in Nazi-occupied Europe might have changed their minds about emigrating. But to no avail.

The Shanghai radio stations broadcast the terrible war news. We were despairing for those left behind. Uncle Leo wrote us from France that he wanted to join us in Shanghai. When he had left for Paris in 1933, it had seemed the best place to be. It was no longer so. Hitler had annexed Austria, marched into the Rhineland, and invaded Poland, and it looked as if France was going to be the next country under the Nazi boot. Leo filed an application with the Paris office of HICEM, while Mutti filed her application with their counterpart in Shanghai. (HICEM is the European equivalent of HIAS.)

To speed matters up, she herself went to the authorities to get the necessary documents and then arranged for Far Eastern HICEM to transfer them to their Marseille office, for Leo was now in a camp in Septfonds. Mutti now breathed a sigh of relief; she had done everything at her end, and Leo would be joining us soon.

Suddenly, Uncle Leo's letters became frantic. Where are the papers? Please do something fast. Mutti ran to HICEM and asked them to check if the papers had gone out. Calm down, they told her, the papers had been mailed; however, the mail was so unreliable these days, it took a lot of time for letters to reach France. So again we waited.

We heard that the most endangered Jews were those who had only residency status, like Leo, rather than French citizenship. Again Mutti pestered HICEM. The documents should have reached their Marseille office by now. "Please check your files."

"Don't get excited, she was told again; everything is under control. Things just take time."

Again, a frantic telegram from Leo: RIKA, PLEASE HELP ME LEAVE FRANCE.

This time Mutti was not going to be placated with words. She demanded to see the director, Meyer Birman. He was busy, she was told. "I will wait," she replied grimly. And so she waited.

Finally, an exasperated official asked her what she wanted. She explained the situation and demanded to see the file as well as the registered mail receipt for the package containing Leo's documents.

Finally, she got in to see Mr. Birman. After hearing her story, he requested Leo's file. As he opened the file, his face blanched. Alarmed, Mutti asked what was the matter. He showed her the papers, all intact, in an envelope. They had never been mailed.

Mutti became hysterical. How could they do this? Why hadn't they checked the file the many times she asked them to? Now, Leo was never going to get out. He was surely doomed. "We will mail them immediately," she was told, "special delivery, registered. Don't worry, even though there has been a delay, everything has been processed and there should be no problem."

This time, Mutti did not trust them. She took the envelope to the Post Office herself and mailed it airmail, special delivery, registered. However, it was too late. HICEM informed us that their office in Marseille was closed and the documents were never delivered.

Mutti walked around in a daze. She kept repeating, over and over, *"Mein Bruder muss denken dass seine Schwester ihn verlassen hat!* (My brother must think that his sister has deserted him!)"

Chapter 21

I adjusted to Shanghai and my new friends rather well. My closest friend was Ellen Salomon, our doctor's daughter. We were the same age and in the same class at the Shanghai Jewish School.

On school days, we would take the tramway, which stopped right in front of our lane. Because this was the first stop, where the tram turned around, we could always get a seat—it usually got very crowded later. When the tram let us off at Seymour Road, there was still a little walk to the school. If we had the money, we would take the electric trolley; if not we would walk, which would take us fifteen to twenty minutes. (The tramway ran on tracks, the trolley was an electric bus powered by overhead cables.)

I joined the British Girl Guides and soon became a patrol leader. I loved the Sunday bonfires and learning to tie all kinds of knots. I learned Morse code and was particularly proficient at semaphoring.

I had also joined the Betar, founded in 1923, by a Russian Zionist, Vladimir (Ze'ev) Jabotinsky (1880–1940), as the youth organization of the Zionist Revisionist Party. The ZRP advocated the building of Israel on a national militaristic basis. Jabotinsky also helped found the Jewish Legion, which fought on the side of the British during the war.

Our group, however, was mostly social. All our meetings would start with the singing of "*Hatikvah*," and then we would sing other Jewish pioneer songs. We would discuss the bravery of the Halutzim, the early pioneers who had gone to Palestine to fulfill Herzl's dream of a Jewish State.

I went swimming at the YMCA and, at school, had my first taste of field hockey, volleyball, and scrimmage, which was played with a round ball and consisted mostly of passing it around to get a goal.

I enjoyed hockey the most, playing center or right field. It was exciting to play in the interschool rivalries, either against the British PTH, or against the French Aurora school. We usually did very well.

In the meantime I won first place ribbons again at the June 1940 track and field event. Again I thrilled my parents by getting my name into the newspaper.

It was difficult for us to get accustomed to the new foods and a new way of cooking. The fact that we had to boil *everything* took away much of the pleasure of eating vegetables and fruit. Indian corn (to Americans plain "corn") was the staple after rice. In Europe corn was only fed to the chickens, so this was a new food for us. For this reason, at first, Mutti wouldn't even consider eating it.

Mutti was never sure if the fish she bought in the market was fresh (she once saw the fish seller smear the gills with blood to make it look fresh), so she would go to the market with a pail and buy the fish live. I soon got used to coming home from school and finding a fish swimming in the bathtub.

Mr. Lifchitz employed a *shochet*, a Jewish ritual slaughterer, to come to the compound every Friday around noon with some chickens, and perform the ritual slaughtering for those of us who wished to purchase chickens for the Sabbath. That way we also knew the chickens were fresh.

I remember the first time I watched this procedure. I had never seen an animal killed, and even though I was repelled seeing an innocent creature slaughtered for food, it amazed me to see how efficiently and quickly this was done by the *shochet*, so that the animal would suffer the least amount of pain.

The typewriter business was thriving, and even though we did not have the luxuries we had known in Germany, and the climate and unsanitary conditions were troubling, life was pretty comfortable. What bothered us chiefly was Vati's health which had hardly improved, and that Omi, who was on her way to Shanghai, would notice how wan he looked.

Chapter 22

I will never forget June 7, 1940, my father's forty-third birthday, when we stood at The Bund waiting for the best birthday present yet—the arrival of the *Conte Verde*, finally bringing Omi to Shanghai.

Our former cook, Edith, had taken care of her till the day of departure, and the Juliusburgers had done the rest. I am sure it could not have been easy for them to travel with a seventy-two-year-old lady, whose longest voyage, so far, had been by train from Jarotschin to Breslau in 1919.

The temperature was about 90 degrees when the boat docked, and here was Omi wearing her *sheitl*, the wig worn by orthodox women, a long black dress with three petticoats, and high-laced black boots, coming down the gangplank. She looked quite a sight, but we were delirious to see her.

"Benno, you don't look well," were the first words out of her mouth. We had hoped she wouldn't notice his color. Even though he was much improved from the jaundice, he still looked a little yellow and very drawn.

When she unpacked, we discovered that she had not only brought all her high boots, long dresses, and several wigs, but also her featherbed, without which she refused to sleep. The featherbed soon got damp and mildewy and had to be discarded, and Mutti finally persuaded her that in this subtropical heat she would be much more comfortable without her wig.

It was the first time that I had seen Omi without it, and it made quite a difference. Her wig was dark brown and parted in the middle, but her real hair was wispy and snow-white. She ended up combing it back and pinning it into a little bun at the nape of her neck.

Now we had to introduce her to Number One Boy and Mah Ling. Omi wanted to do all the cooking and baking, for she excelled in both. At this point it was impossible to teach her a new language, yet she could not do anything without Boy or Mah Ling.

Boy and Omi started a strange love-hate relationship. Many a time I would come home from school and find the two of them screaming at each other, Boy in Chinese or pidjin and Omi in German. Yet, in their own way, they even got to understand what each wanted from the other. When Mutti would come home from the office, the first words out of Boy's mouth would usually be, "Ole missy make lots walla-walla today." It seemed that each time she told him to do something, he would tell her "bahm-by," which she understood soon enough to mean "by and by" in pidjin English and then she learned that "maskee," meant never mind.

The news that continued to come out of Europe was disastrous. Shanghai radio kept us informed of the news in several languages: English, German, French, Russian, as well as Japanese, and Chinese.

In rapid succession, Denmark, Norway, the Netherlands, and Belgium fell under the Nazi jackboot. Then, calamitously, we heard of the fall of France and the hasty retreat of the British from the continent. To bring matters home, it was known that the Nazis had a Fifth Column operating within the confines of Shanghai itself.

Chapter 23

Vati's health still vacillated. Some days he would be fine, yet he had never entirely shaken off the jaundice. In early 1941, Mutti finally persuaded him to have a full physical checkup. He came home beaming.

"What did I tell you?" he exulted. "Dr. Salomon says I have the constitution of a twenty-year-old. Everything checks out. I just have to take it easy a little bit and cut down on my smoking."

My music-loving parents—in Breslau they were always off to concerts and the opera—kept up with cultural events in Shanghai, and on the evening of February 22, they had opera tickets. Because Vati had looked very drawn all week, Mutti suggested he take a nap in the afternoon, so he would be rested for the evening. Reluctantly, he did so. As she woke him to get dressed, he jumped up from the couch and suddenly winced with pain.

"*Verdammt*, I jumped up so quickly, I twisted my ankle," he exclaimed. Mutti ran over with some ice and an elastic bandage, but even so, the foot remained swollen, so she suggested they stay home and rest the ankle.

"Nonsense, it's only a sprained ankle. I am not staying home."

"Well, at least let the doctor look at it," suggested Mutti.

"Not necessary, just help me get dressed, or we'll be late."

So Mutti helped Vati get dressed. When he tried to put his bandaged foot into the shoe, he literally blanched with the pain. So Mutti gave him Omi's cane to lean on, and they departed.

The next day Vati was still in pain and lay in bed with the foot raised. Friends came by to see how he was feeling. From the kitchen I overheard one of them say to Mutti, "I never thought I'd see the day when Benno Popielarz would be walking with a cane. But he really looked ill last night."

On Monday, when I came home from school, Mutti shushed me and told me to be quiet for Vati was sleeping. By Tuesday, over Vati's vehement protests, she called Dr. Salomon, for it was obvious that his condition was more serious than just a sprained ankle. He was also running a low-grade fever again.

Dr. Salomon consulted with some of the specialists, an or-thopedist, a hematologist, and the tropical disease expert, who had treated Vati previously. The orthopedist said there was no fracture and the sprain would heal by itself; in the meantime, Vati should stay off the foot as much as possible.

The hematologist took a blood specimen to try to come up with a diagnosis.

The tropical disease specialist thought that possibly Vati had never gotten over the jaundice and that the trauma of the sprain might be the cause of the fever.

Dr. Salomon prescribed sulfa and aspirin and admonished Vati to stay put in bed. And for once Vati listened.

By Thursday he was feeling much better and got out of bed for a little while. Friday he felt well enough to want to go to his office, but Mutti suggested he stay in for the weekend; Yih Ah had everything under control. It was great to eat Sabbath dinner together and to see Vati well again.

Saturday morning, Mutti decided to stay home with Vati instead of attending synagogue services, for she didn't trust him not to get out of bed. I decided to stay home also. At one point, I heard Vati calling her to help him get out of bed—he had to go to the toilet. I ran into the room. There was Tasso at the edge of the bed and Mutti in the process of helping Vati get up. Then, suddenly, he slumped against her.

"*Benno, was ist los?*" she cried. Only there was no answer.

"Quickly get Dr. Salomon. Tell him your father is very sick, to come immediately."

I ran out of the apartment and up the long flight of stairs to Dr. Salomon's office which was a room in his apartment. He literally flew down the stairs and into Vati's bedroom. They wouldn't let me go in. Finally, Mutti and the doctor came out of the room, and Mutti was crying.

"Evelinchen, *Vati ist tot.*"

My handsome, fun-loving Vati was dead. He had died in Mutti's arms. It was March 1, 1941, three months short of his forty-fourth birthday. My parents had been married just twelve short years.

His mother had to be told. I knocked on Omi's door and said that

Mutti wanted to see her. When she walked in, Dr. Salomon explained as gently as he could. "Benno, *mein Kind*," she cried. Both her children gone. One in Paraguay, whom she hadn't heard from for a long time, and Benno, the apple of her eye, dead in Shanghai.

For religious reasons no autopsy was performed. Seven physicians had treated him at various times—specialists in tropical diseases, infectious diseases, a hematologist, a gastroenterologist and internist, and our family physician. The final cause of death was a pulmonary embolism, however, there was a strong possibility that when he was so badly wounded on the battlefield, there was organ damage which had never been diagnosed. When he developed intractable diarrhea in Buchenwald which was never treated, it may have been from the contaminated whale meat. This left him in a debilitated state from which he was unable to recover fully before undertaking the long sea voyage. Liver damage was not ruled out, particularly since he developed jaundice or infectious hepatitis. He may also have suffered from a touch of malaria. In his weakened condition, the Shanghai climate didn't help. Had we been able to emigrate to a "friendlier" climate, and more modern medical facilities, he might have had a chance. We will never know, of course!

The funeral arrangements were made by the Chevra Kadisha for burial at the Columbia Road cemetery.

Mr. Lifschitz was beside himself. He immediately arranged for the services to take place in the little *shul* in the compound. It was standing room only. My parents were very popular.

I still remember the slatted pine coffin as it was brought out the front door of our apartment. I was standing outside with Omi, Mutti, Boy, and Mah Ling, who were also in shock, and wailing according to the Chinese custom. The fact that Vati was so young made his death seem all the more tragic. Omi was in such bad shape that Mutti and Dr. Salomon decided that she should not go to the cemetery and asked me to stay at home with her. I wanted to go badly, but they wouldn't let me. To this day I miss not having gone.

Mutti later told me that all the firms Vati had been doing business with sent representatives to the funeral and huge floral wreaths. Yih Ah stood at the grave with tears running down his cheeks. He sent the largest wreath. Even though Jewish custom in the diaspora does not permit flowers at a grave, Mutti didn't want to offend anyone, so she requested that the wreaths be laid next to the grave rather than on it.

The whole Jewish Company of the SVC had come in uniform, and some of the men were pallbearers. A bugler played taps.

Then there was a problem of saying Kaddish, which was to be said for the dead by his brother, Uncle Leo, in Asuncion. Omi had received letters occasionally from him, in which he always told her that money, in the form of a bank draft, was on the way for her, but the promised draft never arrived. Yet, when Vati died, and Mutti cabled him to recite Kaddish, we expected some reply. When none came, she was faced with the prospect of paying some stranger to recite this prayer, and she didn't want to do that, so she petitioned the rabbi for permission for me to undertake this obligation for my father, there being no son. After much thought, the rabbi agreed that an exception could be made, because I was under twelve years old. I recited the Kaddish at the synagogue during the service, and thereafter every morning before school, as well as every evening, for the full eleven months of mourning.

The three of us, Mutti, Omi, and I sat *shiva* during the seven days of mourning. Every morning and evening during that period, a service was conducted in the apartment. All my classmates and all my parents' friends came to pay their respects. I wore a navy blue dress and a blue ribbon in my braided hair. The dress was torn at the collar as a sign of mourning.

On the last day of the *shiva* period, I didn't feel too well. Mutti thought it was from all the excitement, but when I broke out in small red blotches, she called Dr. Salomon.

"Measles," he proclaimed. So for the next few weeks I had to remain in a darkened room. When I went back to school, I felt that my whole life had changed. I had always been a carefree extrovert; I was now a shy, reserved, unhappy ten-year-old.

Chapter 24

As soon as the *shiva* period was over, Mutti called the Shanghai Volunteer Corps to pick up Vati's guns and uniforms. She did not want to keep them in the apartment a moment longer than absolutely necessary. The only item she held onto was a blue, Nehru-style cap he had worn at his SVC meetings. It still is in my possession.

Tasso kept running around the apartment, sniffing and whining unhappily, looking for Vati. He still insisted on sleeping at the foot of Vati's side of the bed. After a while, Mutti couldn't take him anymore. The little dog reminded her too much of Vati. She gave him to Yih Ah, who promised to take care of a living memento of his beloved boss.

I was very unhappy when Tasso was given away, and Mutti finally relented and let me have a puppy from a litter in the compound. It was a small smooth-haired terrier, with one blue eye and one brown eye. I refused to have his tail bobbed because I didn't want him in pain. I named him Duke.

Vati had run the typewriter business with Yih Ah as his assistant. With him gone, Yih Ah could not handle the shop by himself. What good did it do for Mutti to bring in new accounts when they could not be expedited. Not being a mechanic herself, she had difficulty estimating the price of a job. Business dropped drastically and suddenly we were in a terrible financial bind.

Mutti, of course, always found a solution. She had Yih Ah train her as a mechanic, and although she still retained his services, from then on she did it all—soliciting customers, making appointments, taking care of the correspondence and bookkeeping, and doing minor repairs. Many a time I would travel with her in a rickshaw during the summer holidays, or after school, helping her lug heavy office machines to and from customers' offices.

As a matter of fact, her customers bent over backward to help her out, and with my knowledge of English and some school French, I was able to help her too, by conversing with many of them.

Mutti then approached my school principal and told him she would be unable to pay my tuition any longer. She was immediately advised that I could continue attending, indefinitely, on a scholarship, that included lunches, until she was able to resume payments.

After reluctantly dismissing Boy, she only retained Mah Ling to take care of the household after renting out my room to a German refugee, a bachelor. I would be sleeping with her. The two front rooms had been rented to the Böhms, a dentist and his wife from Hamburg, right after we moved in, in order to defray some of our expenses. We retained the large room which now became the living-dining- and bedroom for us. We still kept our private kitchen and bathroom, and with the above arrangements, Mutti explained to me, we would manage and be living rent-free. Omi lived separately next door, with a private entrance to her room.

She had gotten very depressed since Vati's death. She wouldn't cook any more and hardly spoke to anyone. Occasionally, I would try to coax her to go for walks, and then all she would talk about was Benno. She would come to eat with us but would fix nothing for herself.

Mutti didn't like the idea that Omi would be alone all day after my summer vacations were over. Her schedule was irregular, for besides managing the repair shop she would be visiting customers at all hours. Through the kind mediation of Mr. Lifschitz, she managed to place Omi in a Russian Jewish old age home, where she would be well taken care of. It helped that Omi spoke Polish, as well as German, for Polish was somewhat similar to Russian, and of course Yiddish was similar to German. The fee wasn't too high, and after selling Vati's clothes and other possessions, Mutti was able to take care of Omi's expenses.

In the meantime, the political situation was getting really sinister. The Germans had attacked the Soviets and were advancing on Moscow. The flow of refugees from western Europe had stopped and suddenly ships carrying Polish refugees began arriving from Japan.

Many of these people had fled Poland after Hitler's invasion, heading east, and had ended up in Russia or on the Trans-Siberian Railroad carrying them even further east. These refugees either had American affidavits and/or steamship tickets for the United States. For this reason they had been granted transit visas by Japan as they waited for their American visas in Kobe. While a decision was awaited from U.S. immigration, Japan kept granting extensions on these transit visas. However, the American visas were not forthcoming. In late spring 1941, they were told that they are being sent to Shanghai to join their fellow refugees.

What next?

RIPO Typewriters had somewhat picked up, when "the other shoe dropped." On Monday morning, December 8, 1941*, the city was rocked by a tremendous explosion that seemed to come from the vicinity of The Bund and the harbor. The Japanese had dynamited and sunk two ships anchored in the Whangpoo, effectively blocking the harbor of Shanghai to any and all outside shipping. Then came the grim news over the radio. A jubilant announcer told his listeners, in five languages, that the victorious Japanese naval air force had attacked a sleeping U.S. Navy at Pearl Harbor, Hawaii, and sunk almost the entire Pacific fleet.

Now it was truly a *world* war, waged on three continents, Europe, Asia, and Africa. And, as in previous centuries, Jews were once again in limbo. With Japan and Germany allied, what effect would it have on us—18,000 stateless Jewish refugees? Had we leaped from the Nazi frying pan into the Japanese fire?

One effect was immediate. All American, British, Dutch, and Belgian businesses were immediately closed down by the Japanese and their nationals were issued red armbands with a large A, B, or N, respectively. Members of British Protectorates were issued pink armbands with the letter X. These armbands had to be worn in public at all times.

A few months later these nationals, except for those issued the pink X, were interned in camps at Lunghwa on the outskirts of Shanghai. Our British school principal, and our British and Dutch teachers were interned, so that we were left mainly with our Russian teachers, plus one new addition: Mr. Kuzuoka had joined the teaching staff of the Shanghai Jewish School. Japanese had been added to our language curriculum.

---

* Because of the International Date Line, this was the same date as December 7 in Hawaii.

All but two of the American staff of the Joint had been recalled to the United States. Laura Margolies, and her colleague Manuel Siegel had stayed on and were still assisting with the soup kitchens in Hongkew.

Ration coupons were issued by the Japanese authorities. Each person's monthly ration consisted of a quarter pound of brown sugar, a quarter pound of butter, and one pound of flour, as well as several coupons for the purchase of cotton fabric. They also issued occupation currency.

It was illegal to possess foreign currency or gold bars, so people started hoarding and hiding. We were not permitted to travel into the suburbs, and overseas mail was restricted to fifty words, which had to be printed on special Red Cross stationery. The same stationery and fifty words were used to communicate with the interned "enemy nationals."

As the occupying forces in Shanghai, the Japanese now ran the city with a strong arm. To ensure that the local population got inoculated, they had nurses, flanked by soldiers, forcibly stop people in the street and immunize them then and there. They also made sure that the rickshaws got sprayed with DDT on a regular basis in order to delouse them.

Except for the severe food shortage that developed—and with it, of course, a flourishing black market—nothing much had changed for the refugees. We were in the same boat as the general population, completely isolated from the rest of the world.

Shanghai's Japanese-issued Occupation currency.

Chapter 25

With most of Mutti's customers now interned, and the rest having no business to transact, the typewriter business which had so recently improved, took a drastic downward turn. No one purchased new machines, and there was little need for servicing, repairs, or rentals. Regretfully, Mutti had to let Yih Ah go, and ran the dwindling business on her own. She made that decision with a heavy heart, for Yih Ah Kung had been a good and loyal employee. She also had to dismiss Mah Ling and I had to do without weekly movies, the occasional leasing of a bicycle, food delicacies, and new clothes. Actually the only movies now available to us were in French, German, Chinese, or Japanese, though some of them had English subtitles. No English-language movies could be shown. All Mutti's income now went for rent, food, transportation, and Omi's keep in the nursing home.

Life had become an endless chore, with few pleasures outside my school sports activities and visits with friends, who were in similar straits.

It was the beginning of 1942, and I was still reciting the daily Kaddish for Vati. There was never any problem getting a *minyan*, a quorum of ten men, for the morning service; however, evenings were a little more difficult.

When it was time for services, my friends and I would start knocking on doors, asking the available men to be part of a *minyan*. Invariably the question would be, "How many do you have?" If we were truthful and admitted we had only five or six men lined up, we would be told, "Let me know when you have nine—then I'll be the tenth." After a while, we learned to tell a white lie. No matter how many men had agreed to come, our answer would always be "nine." During my whole mourning period, we rarely failed to have a *minyan*.

Spring, 1942. The censored war news on the radio and in the newspapers described only German and Japanese victories. We were warned that Shanghai would probably be bombed by the Americans, and an air raid warning system was activated. We had periodic blackouts, but no underground shelters were possible because of the topography.

The Japanese had dug curbside trenches into which we were told to duck should we be caught in an air raid while outdoors. School continued without interruption. The portraits of the King and Queen were replaced with that of Emperor Hirohito and his Empress, and the Union Jack was replaced with the Rising Sun. We were no longer permitted to sing "God Save the King," instead we had to listen to a recording of *"Kimigayo"* (Reign of the Emperor), the Japanese national anthem. However, we still sang *"Hatikvah."*

We were not happy studying Japanese, but were told we could not be promoted if we failed that subject. We gave poor Mr. Kuzuoka a very hard time indeed. He could not hear too well, and his English was not too good either. We had to treat him with the same respect as we treated the other teachers, and whenever he came into the classroom and we would rise, he would say in his heavily accented English, "Shittee down shittee down." I don't think he ever caught on why that would get us so hysterical.

He was shortly replaced by a younger teacher, very suave and well spoken, Mr. Suzuki, who was able to discipline us much better. We were taught the alphabet, reading and writing, as well as vocabulary and grammar.

As we started our winter semester, we were told that the Japanese authorities would be converting our school building into a hospital in case of American bombardments when additional hospital space would be needed. Classrooms were found for us in the business district of St. George, at the Shanghai (Russian) Jewish Club, across the street from the German Consulate.

We now had to give up some of our classes and activities. No sports, for the Race Course had become the parade ground of the Japanese military. No swimming, for the YMCA was now a Japanese Officers' Club. No playground, no library, no laboratory, no gym. The classes were conducted around the card and billiard tables, and when school was let out, the men would be waiting impatiently at the door, with cards and billiard cues in hand. Ironically, when we sang *"Hatikvah"* before classes every morning, it would be in full view of the swastika fluttering in the breeze from the roof of the German Consulate across the street.

Chapter 26

As a refugee community, we were still left pretty much to our own devices. By scrimping and saving, as well as selling some more of our personal possessions, Mutti managed to eke out a meager living. Even though having tenants in the apartment took care of our rent, on the other hand the displaced school was no longer able to provide its students with lunch. Many of us would share our lunches.

We also shared our tramway tickets. One student would buy a ticket and, after it was punched, would pass it surreptitiously along to another student, and so on. In such fashion perhaps three students could ride on one ticket. If the conductor caught on, those of us without the ticket would get off at the next stop and walk the remainder of the way—or perhaps pull the same trick again on the next tram.

All my friends still had two working parents, which allowed them to be a little better off financially than I was. They were really good to me. I was often invited for dinner to their homes. Two of my friends in the compound, who were also my classmates, were Ellen Salomon and Ethel Shmulewitz.

Ethel's father had been a rabbi at the Mirrer Yeshiva in Poland. The family, consisting of Ethel, her mother, and a number of siblings, had been among the Polish refugees in transit in Kobe who were subsequently sent to Shanghai.

I had never met anyone quite that Orthodox, and it was a revelation. Ethel, a very pretty girl, was extremely bright and personable. She had beautiful blond braids which she would braid tightly before sundown on Friday because she could not comb her hair on the Sabbath. Even though we were kosher, she would not eat in my home because we were not as Orthodox as her family.

However, I would be invited to the Shmulewitz home frequently. The Mirrer Yeshiva in Brooklyn managed to transmit money to their members among the refugee colony in Shanghai, affording them a slightly higher standard of living than the rest of us had.

Ellen and I used to do a lot of roller skating. It was especially fun in the compound, for we could skate around the big planter, and there was no traffic. Then, one day, Ellen tripped and fell right in front of our door. I tried to raise her up and saw that her arm did not look right. I ran up to get her father, and they took her to the hospital. She had broken her arm very badly, and it must have been poorly set, because when the cast came off, her arm was crooked. Mutti took one look at Ellen's arm, and took away my roller skates.

"What did I do?" I objected. "I didn't fall, Ellen did."

"But you might fall, and I can't afford to have you in the hospital and hurt."

So, there went one more pleasure. Now all I could do was skip rope and run—all very boring activities.

Two other friends had also come from Poland by way of Japan—Chaya Ambaras and Susie Kushner. I felt a kinship with them, because Omama Miriam had come from there. They lived in the French Concession and were in my class at the Shanghai Jewish School. Susie excelled in drawing which was my weakest subject in school, and she would always help me out in class and with our drawing homework.

Another friend was Ruth Katz, who had been with us on the *Hakozaki Maru*. One day she went on a school outing to Hangchow and ate a tomato from the vine. (We had always been admonished never to eat anything raw.) She developed cholera very quickly, and even though she had been inoculated against the disease, she died within a few days. She was twelve years old. It reinforced all the warnings not to eat any uncooked foods.

This tragedy shook the whole school, and students turned out en masse for the funeral. What made it particularly poignant, Ruth was an only child and her mother was past child-bearing age.

Chapter 27

It was the end of 1942, and very disquieting rumors were making the rounds.

We are going to be deported. Where to, no one knew. Someone had heard that there were Gestapo agents in Shanghai, who were probably plotting something. What were they plotting? Who saw them? Then someone heard that we are going to be put on little ships and set adrift in the Yangtze River. Rumors, rumors. No one knew where they started, but, nevertheless, we knew something was up.

I still visited Omi at the home about two or three afternoons a week. She was always happy to see me and would tell me stories of Vati's youth and her home in Jarotschin. She insisted that one of her servants, Marienka, had had twenty-four children and was still able to work for her. When Vati was born, she said, the baby wouldn't wait for the midwife to arrive, he just "popped out." I loved these stories about Vati whom I only remembered as a fun person to be with, but knew very little about his youth.

One Thursday afternoon during my visit, she told me that she had dreamed that Benno was calling her to join him and that she had told him she would, very, very soon. It scared me, for it seemed uncanny that Vati would be speaking to her. I told Mutti about this, but she said it was only a dream. People often dreamed what was in their thoughts during the day.

Vati's second *Yahrzeit*, the anniversary of his death, was on Sunday, the second of *Adar Rishon.*

As had been done the year before, we arranged for services in our apartment. It was Saturday afternoon, and the rabbi had just concluded *mincha*, the afternoon service, and was waiting for sundown, which signified the next day on the Jewish calendar, to conduct *maariv*, the evening service, at which time I would be reciting the Kaddish. Suddenly the telephone rang. Mutti answered it, spoke for a few moments, then hung up and came into the room.

"That was the old age home. Omi just died—peacefully in her sleep," she announced sadly. "She took her regular afternoon nap and just never woke up."

The rabbi looked at his watch, it was six o'clock, not yet sundown. Omi had died on the first of *Adar Rishon*, February 6, 1943, just one day short of two years after her son's death, from which she had really never recovered. She was seventy-four years old.

I remembered our conversation, just two days before, and wondered, did Vati actually summon her? I would never know.

The Columbia Road cemetery, where Vati was buried, was full. She was buried on the new Point Road cemetery in Hongkew. Even though she felt it would be useless, Mutti nevertheless again sent a telegram to Uncle Leo in Asuncion, this time, because of the war, via the Red Cross, advising him of his mother's death. As before, there was no reply, so Mutti paid a rabbi to recite the Kaddish prayer for Omi for the required eleven months.

(After the war we tried to contact my uncle in Asuncion. No one had ever heard of him. He, his wife and my cousin Lore had simply disappeared.)

Chapter 28

PROCLAMATION
CONCERNING RESTRICTION OF RESIDENCE AND BUSINESS OF STATELESS REFUGEES

I.   Due to military necessity, places of residence and business of the stateless refugees in the Shanghai area shall hereafter be restricted to the undermentioned area in the International Settlement. East of the line connecting Chaoufoong Road, Muirhead Road and Dent Road; West of Yangtzepoo Creek; North of the line connecting East Seward Road and Wayside Road; and South of the boundary on the International Settlement.

II. The stateless refugees presently residing and/or carrying on business in the district other than the above area shall remove their places of residence and/or business into the area designated above by May 18, 1943.
Permission must be obtained from the Japanese authorities for the transfer, sale, purchase or lease of rooms, houses, shops or any other establishments, which are situated outside the designated are and are now being occupied or used by the stateless refugees.

III. Persons other than the stateless refugees shall not remove into the area mentioned in Article I without permission of the Japanese authorities.

IV. Persons who will have violated this Proclamation or obstructed its reenforcement shall be liable to severe punishment.

Commander-in-Chief
of the Imperial Japanese Army in the Shanghai Area.

Commander-in-Chief
of the Imperial Japanese Navy in the Shanghai Area.

This proclamation, printed in all the newspapers and announced on all the radio stations, took us totally by surprise. The term "stateless" struck a note of fear and despair into the hearts of the refugee colony. "Stateless" meant all refugees who had entered Shanghai *after* 1937, for none of us had valid passports any longer.

It is interesting to note that the words "Jew" or "ghetto" were never used in the proclamation. But "designated area" was obviously a euphemism for "ghetto." Thus, approximately 10,000 of us who had homes and businesses outside Hongkew had to relocate a second time into a crowded, squalid area, encompassing a little less than one square mile already populated by over 100,000 people, 8,000 of them refugees who had been living there since their arrival in Shanghai. They, of course, had the advantage of remaining in their homes, while the rest of us had to search for almost non-existing housing. We had three months in which to relocate.

Shortly after Pearl Harbor, the Joint withdrew its authorization for loans to support the refugee community. This was a terrible setback for Laura Margolies. The Japanese realized that this money was desperately needed and were willing to accept funds on behalf of the refugees. But the Joint was afraid that if they honored an extension of the loan commitment, it might be construed as a circumvention of the Anglo-American Trading with the Enemy Act, thereby compromising American Jewry.

Laura managed to obtain some small loans on behalf of the Joint to keep the soup kitchens going in Hongkew, but in January 1943, just before the ghetto proclamation was issued, she, and her colleague Manuel Siegel were interned by the Japanese. (They were both repatriated to the United States in December.)

"What are we going to do now?" despaired Mutti. "We were just about able to keep our heads above water, and now this. It's a mercy that Omi died before this calamity."

Mutti wanted to avoid moving to one of the *Heime*, the group residence for really poor refugees, so she got together with the Fischers, the Rings, and Dr. Böhm (our tenant at Avenue Joffre, whose wife had just died), and suggested we all chip in to buy one of the Chinese houses in the ghetto.

After much searching, for there was a minimum of private housing available, a two story, four-room house was located, at 498/8 Ward Road, and purchased.

SACRA, acronym for Shanghai Ashkenazi Collaborating Relief Association, had also established a compound in the ghetto, renting rooms to refugees. Chaya and Susie were moving into one of the SACRA buildings.

Once more we were packing up our much-diminished belongings. Mutti sold all but the absolute necessities to a Japanese family, who took over the lease of our apartment. She also sold Vati's stamp collection which she had been holding on to so desperately; the proceeds paid for our share of the ghetto quarters, the moving costs, and the illegal black market purchase of three gold bars. She showed me where she was hiding them.

"These gold bars are our last resort to keep us from starvation," she told me. "Never divulge to anyone that we have them and where they are. I am only telling you now, in case anything happens to me." She had sewn them into one of her silk dresses which she knew she'd never wear in the ghetto.

Anyone who had emigrated to Shanghai before 1937 was not affected by the Japanese proclamation, so Mr. Lifschitz, as well as all the other Russians, Jewish and non-Jewish, could remain where they were. However, he was now sadly losing all his refugee tenants, who had been one happy family. We were quickly replaced by Japanese families.

The Japanese also issued deferments and extensions for ghetto relocations. Certain professionals—i.e., doctors, dentists, some rabbis—were given deferments to stay out of the ghetto, while people who had difficulty finding housing in Hongkew were given three-month extensions to give them a little time to relocate. (In this and other things, the Japanese were far more reasonable than their Nazi counterparts in Europe—or so we learned later.)

Dr. Salomon received a deferment and stayed in the compound. I would now see my friend Ellen only at school.

During the first week of May, Mr. Lifschitz threw a big farewell party on the grounds of the compound. We did not know if we'd ever see each other again.

PART III

Hongkew
1943–1945

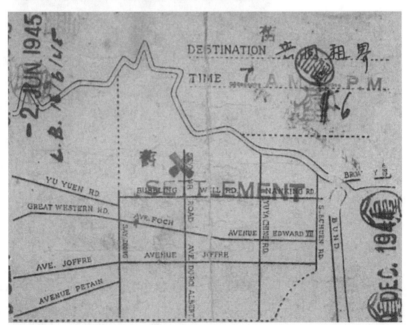

Author's ghetto pass. Renewal dates are marked on front as well as back, which includes a notation into which area bearer is permitted to travel. Note last renewal date of September 3, 1945—our day of liberation.

Chapter 29

Mutti had liquidated the typewriter shop on Szechuen Road, just holding on to three of her typewriters, an Olivetti portable, an Underwood, and a Remington, hoping to be able to rent them out. And she kept all her tools. We moved during the first week of May with the other three families.

The house was in a narrow alley off the main center lane. All the houses in the alley were attached, and each had two entrances—one from the back and one from the front. The front allowed entrance into a small, damp area, with a cement floor, a sink with one faucet, sporadically supplying cold water only. There was no flush toilet, and we were expected to use the "honey pot" that the other inhabitants of the lane were accustomed to using.

The honey pot was a portable toilet, and every morning a coolie would come around to collect the contents, which he would then pour into a large container in his wagon, and the Chinese women would scrub their pails in the alley with a stiff straw brush and cold water.

We did not want to use the honey pot and had arranged for the installation of a flush toilet for the ten occupants of our house. Not only did we have to get special permission for this installation, but we also had to compensate the honey pot coolie who lost revenue thereby.

Our precious toilet was located in a tiny room right next to the front door. It had a little window. However, because the floor was of unfinished and uneven cement, partly muddy, the space was always dank and mildewy. I will never forget the stench. Big, fat, red spiders, cockroaches, centipedes, and other vermin happily congregated in that little room. We always took our spray container of Flit with us and tried to do our business in a hurry. No one wanted to spend an extra unnecessary moment in there. We consoled ourselves with the thought that this was at least more tolerable than the alternative.

Because the house had no bath or shower, we had a sink installed, with one cold water faucet, in everyone's room. Cooking would be done individually; a section of everyone's quarters would be sectioned off to serve as a private kitchen.

There was no gas, only electricity, which was prohibitively expensive as well as curtailed. We did our cooking on a little Chinese stove stoked with little egg-shaped coals that could either be purchased or made by ourselves out of coal dust mixed with water. A rather messy job, but cheaper that the ready-made variety. To start a fire, we lighted newspapers and kept the flame alive by constant fanning.

Because it took a long time to heat and boil water in such fashion, we purchased our hot or boiling water from the hot water stand located at the lane's entrance. For that we needed two pails. One we marked "hot water" and the other "boiling water" so as not to confuse one with the other, for the boiling water, which was more expensive, could then be used as drinking water.

The accommodations were apportioned according to the size of the family and its use. The Fischers were four people and received a large ground-floor room, which they partitioned into two rooms and a kitchen.

One flight up, on either side of the stairwell, were our quarters and Dr. Böhm's. Even though he was just one person, he moved into the other large room right above the Fischers' quarters, where he set up his dental practice, curtaining off the area that served as his bedroom, dining room, waiting room, and examination/treatment room. The front part of the room was partitioned off into a kitchen, which we were sharing with him. Now, Mutti congratulated herself on her foresight in having our Avenue Joffre cupboards constructed as single-standing units. They served perfectly as partitions for the kitchen, which also contained a sink and a small icebox.

Our quarters consisted of a tiny room with a cement floor called the "meter room," for it contained the electric meter, which was read once a month. Because Mutti and I were the smallest family, we had agreed to take this room, for which we had paid proportionately less as our share in the house. It contained a sink, a small table, a chair, and one of our cupboards from the French Concession. The room also had a small window overlooking the alley. Because the alley was so narrow, no sunlight filtered through, and the room was always dark.

Our light consisted of a 25-watt naked lightbulb hanging above the table, and when our small allotment of electricity ran out—and also to save money—we used a kerosene lamp, for candles were much too expensive. When we could not afford the kerosene, Mutti used little pieces of metal into which she punched a little hole; a small wick was stuck through the opening, and the metal was then placed on a dish containing some cooking oil. When the wick was lighted, it gave us some light. As a matter of fact, these little metal disks also served as our Sabbath and holiday candlesticks. For *Hanukkah*, we fashioned nine of the disks, one to serve as the *shamash* and the others to be lighted during the eight-day festival.

We knew none of our electric appliances were going to work in Shanghai, so we brought with us an old-fashioned iron with a "heating bolt." We never had to use it in the French Concession, but it now served a dual purpose. After heating the bolt on our little stove, it also heated our bed on cold nights.

Our window curtain, which also served as our blackout curtain, was a tablecloth that we had brought with us from Germany. The window panes, as well as all the panes in the house, were crisscrossed with tape in order to contain glass shards in the event of a bombardment. Store decorators became quite ingenious with such tape, in a variety of colors, creating interesting designs for their shop windows.

One flight up, right above Dr. Böhm's room, was a large attic room with a sloping roof. The Rings moved into that room.

Three steps up from there was our access to the roof, a flat surface, to which we would bring our chairs on hot summer nights, and I would bring my friends. Our laundry would also be hung there. Looking out over the roof, we would see long lines of colorful, confetti-like laundry hung out to dry by the other residents of the alley. We would also do our cooking on that roof.

When our windows were open, which was almost all year except during the monsoon season or on very cold wintry days, we heard the whine of the Chinese music. The unfamiliar sound grated on our ears, and we had much difficulty sleeping.

Many of the native inhabitants of the lane would take their sleeping mats out onto the street on particularly hot and humid summer nights. When you were taking a walk, you had to exercise extreme care not to trip over a heavy sleeper.

School was now very far away, at the other end of town, and it took anywhere from one to three hours to get there. Many parents were concerned about letting their children travel such a distance, particularly under wartime conditions, and enrolled them in the Kadoorie School, which was situated in the ghetto. I prevailed on Mutti to allow me to continue at the SJS because many of my friends, who were not ghetto dwellers, were there. These were the Sephardim and Russians who were allowed to remain in their domiciles. Only the Sephardim with British passports were interned.

Chapter 30

The ghetto exits were guarded, on a rotating basis, by Japanese sentries, Russian policemen, and Sikhs, who had always been part of the regular police force under the British. Refugee members of the foreign Pao Chia, the auxiliary police organized by the Japanese in 1942, also served as sentries.

A Bureau for Stateless Refugees had been set up at 70 Muirhead Road, headed by Tsutomo Kubota. Kubota hired two men named Ghoya and Okura to administer a pass system, under which we would be permitted to leave the ghetto environs. A blue, or seasonal pass, required renewal every three months, while a pink pass required monthly renewal. This pass consisted of a card with a photograph, stating the sectors of the city the bearer would be permitted to travel to, and a little metal badge with the Chinese character *T'ung*—(May pass)—which had to be worn at all times outside the ghetto area. If it was removed, and the individual was stopped by Japanese occupation soldiers, there could be trouble.The pass, even if valid, would be confiscated, never to be renewed, and the individual could end up in jail. Curfew for return into the ghetto was 6:00 P.M.

I immediately filed an application for a blue pass, so that I could continue attending the Shanghai Jewish School at St. George. I queued up with Susie and Chaya, who were also continuing at SJS, to be interviewed by Mr. Ghoya, who was in charge of giving out the blue passes. Everyone was nervous, for stories had been going around that he was not a very pleasant person. However, that Mr. Okura, who was handling the pink passes, was said to be far worse.

After an hour on line, Susie, Chaya and I were finally ushered in to see Mr. Ghoya. He was a little man, about five feet tall, probably in his fifties, who had been given the awesome responsibility to grant passes to refugees wanting to leave the ghetto temporarily, and such importance had gone to his head. He gave himself the title—"King of the Jews."

So here I was, standing in front of this "King of the Jews," quivering, for I had just seen him slap the face of a six-foot-tall applicant, while denying him a pass.

He glanced at me over his spectacles. "Why don't you go to school here?" he inquired.

"I've been attending the Shanghai Jewish School since 1939, and I do not wish to change schools after all these years, sir," I replied.

He mumbled something under his breath while I got more and more nervous. What if he hits me? I was thinking. What if he won't give me a pass?

After a moment that seemed like an hour, he called his refugee secretary over to him. "Prepare a pass for this child, a blue pass, for travel to the Shanghai Jewish School and back."

I had my precious pass, which would be valid until June. I didn't have to go to the Kadoorie School, and I didn't have to go back to Ghoya till the new semester in September. During the summer vacations, I would remain in the ghetto. I pinned on my little blue tag and ran home, exhilarated, to tell Mutti that I had gotten the precious pass and that Susie and Chaya had also gotten theirs.

When I returned, at the end of August, for my next renewal, Ghoya happened to come out to see how many people were on line. When he saw a number of school children, he told us to come to the head of the line: "You children have to go to school. No waiting on line." We never had a problem getting our renewals promptly.

Not so with the others. Many had a very hard time getting a pass. People were told to come back, time and time again, and even then they would not get a pass for the area that they wanted. If a man was tall, and Ghoya was in a bad mood, he could count on getting slapped. However, in all fairness to Ghoya, after all it was wartime, and although he was mean and nasty and belligerent at times, we had never heard of him injuring anyone. And the majority of applicants who could prove to his satisfaction that they needed to make a living outside the ghetto, were issued passes.

Mr. Okura, on the other hand, who was mostly in charge of short-term, or one-day passes, was much rougher. He occasionally sent people to jail if he didn't like their answers to his questions or decided they were lying to him. The jails were rat- and louse-infested, a sure way to contract typhus.

As a matter of fact, we did have such a tragedy among the refugee colony. There were about forty Polish yeshiva students who had petitioned the Japanese for an extension of time for removal into the ghetto. They received one extension but were told firmly that, after their three months were up, they would have to move. When, after three months, they did not move and applied for another extension, the Japanese authorities became very angry and warned them that they would be granted just one more extension and that would be it. Thinking they could get away with it a third time, they did not move. The authorities were now fed up. All forty were put in jail, where most of them contracted typhus and a number perished. We couldn't help but feel that sadly they had brought it on themselves. Had they moved when they were supposed to, like everyone else, they might have lived. There was a mass funeral.

Chapter 31

Mutti had to find new ways to earn money. She handed out flyers at the Jewish Community Center and in various little shops, saying that she was a typewriter mechanic, available for servicing, and renting out typewriters. She also advertised in the local newspaper. She managed to pick up a few customers, but it wasn't enough to support us.

Enterprising, as ever, she came up with an idea. Mutti knew her way around sections of the Settlement that were not too popular with other whites. With her limited knowledge of Chinese and pidjin English, she had established a rapport with Chinese peddlers, who sold sundries, either from pushcarts or on floor mats, in the back alleys of Nanking Road, The Bund, Peking Road, Szechuen Road, Bubbling Well Road, and the environs of the Race Course. From them she could purchase belts, silk stockings, scarves, sunglasses, handkerchiefs, wallets, etc., and if she could secret them somehow and bring them back into the ghetto, the refugee peddlers on Tongshan Road would retail them for her on consignment.

But everything depended on getting a pass—any pass.

She contacted some of her former French customers in the French Concession, and asked them for letters of recommendation specifying that she was still doing business with them. They were most cooperative, so she filed a Special Pass application with Ghoya's office. She had to convince him that she was a bonafide typewriter mechanic with clients outside the ghetto.

The refugees queueing up for their passes always tried to gauge Ghoya's mood. The Pao Chia, and some of the other refugees who had obtained clerical positions within the Pass Bureau, would come down the line and whisper, "today he is particularly annoyed with men. Come back tomorrow." Or, "wait till he's had lunch, maybe he'll be in a better mood." That was about as much as they could help those waiting on line.

As Mutti waited, she got more and more nervous: What is he going to think of a female typewriter mechanic? He will never believe me.

Ghoya scanned the application. "You, mechanic?" he asked.

"Yes, sir. I am a widow. My husband was a mechanic, but he died. I have only one child going to school. I need money for food."

"How you take typewriter to French Concession? Very heavy for woman."

Mutti had anticipated that question. She would use the same method of transportation she had always used, she replied, the tramway or rickshaw. And to convince him that she knew her business, she took out her RIPO business card, and explained to Ghoya, who was now listening attentively, that RIPO was a combination of her first and last names and that the business had always been hers. She had done the accounts and had been Vati's assistant while he was alive and then had continued to run the business on her own after his death. She just wanted to keep her business and service her customers outside the ghetto, as before.

Ghoya heard her out. He looked impressed but still doubtful. "Where is your repair shop now?" he wanted to know.

"Right here in Hongkew, at 498/8 Ward Road, sir."

Finally, the magic words: "I will give you a pink pass, but only for the French Concession. You will have to return for renewal within one month."

Mutti breathed a sigh of relief. "Oh, thank you, sir. Thank you very much." She had had very little hope that her plea would earn her the coveted pass, for of course it was all lies, a desperate effort to survive in the ghetto.

She had never intended to lug typewriters back and forth and repair them at home. The distance between the French Concession and the ghetto was too great. She would have to cross half the ghetto to catch the trolley, and she would then have to change tramways twice. The rickshaw would have been the only possible way for her to go, for the coolie would carry the heavy machines for her, but she would not always be able to afford a rickshaw. Also, in the cramped ghetto quarters, it would be difficult for her to service the machines. Benzine, used for cleaning, was very flammable, and the smell was strong. The one or two typewriters that she serviced, she took up to the roof.

But if her former customers were willing to let her service the machines in their offices, then she could do it. All she would have to carry with her would be her tool box; that she could manage.

She asked for a pass only to the French Concession and not to the Settlement as well, because Ghoya seldom granted passes for both sectors. However, the pass for the French Concession allowed her to cross the Settlement, which had to be traversed to get to the French Concession. If by chance she was stopped by a Japanese soldier, she would tell him that she was on her way to customers in the French Concession and had just stopped to buy typewriter supplies. Her plan was to carry her tool kit and her portable Olivetti as proof. She knew she would be taking a chance, but she was willing to risk it.

From Monday to Friday, she left early in the morning, right after seeing me off to school. She returned with her wares, usually before I came home, because she did not want me to return to an empty room. Occasionally, on a Friday or a Saturday night, she would work as a hostess in a community restaurant/kitchen. Besides her small pay, we would also both get a free meal.

Always a Zionist, she had still remained active in the Women's International Zionist Organization (WIZO), which continued to function in the ghetto. In 1944 Mutti was elected president.

During this period she also contemplated buying into a partnership in a notions store. After trying it out for a couple of months, even with my helping out after school, she realized that it would take too long to become profitable, so she had to decide against this venture.

In the meantime, the food situation was still deteriorating. Our sugar, bread, and flour rations were very meager.

Mutti bought some cotton with our ration tickets, and one of the refugee dressmakers made a skirt and dress for me. From her trips into the city, she managed to bring home some thin belts, which the Chinese shoemaker sewed onto a leather sole, and made sandals for me. I painted the straps with blue, black, or red ink, but had to make sure never to wear them in the rain!

The bread that we bought with our ration tickets contained bits of straw that we had to pull out before eating. It was baked with lumpy, grey flour, which was cheaper than the white, so that we were able to obtain more bread with our coupon. Buying bread from the refugee grocer, who worked out of his room, rather than from the bakery, also was cheaper. Many of the refugees had set up shop in their cramped living quarters.

Mutti also bought the grey flour for baking. She would try to bake at least one challah every other week. Once a month, she baked her specialty, and my favorite, *Streuselkuchen.* After she kneaded the dough, she let it rise in the bed under our blanket. Then I carried it three blocks to the bake shop where, for a small sum, they would bake it in their oven.

Occasionally, we would be able to afford some salami, which we bought from another home shop. They sold it by the slice, and Mutti would buy two or three slices at a time, depending on whether she had had a good week. Because we were quite friendly with these people, I knew that if I went along, I would get a free slice. The rest would be our lunch for most of the week.

When Mutti had a little extra money, she bought an egg, with which she made a very special dessert. She beat the whites, combined them with the yellow, then added some vanilla and brown sugar. Sometimes, she would be able to buy a little bit of cocoa to add to the concoction.

She then discovered that mixing peanut butter with syrup would make it go a long way. Spread on a slice of bread, it tasted quite good. We would mix about three ounces of peanut butter with the same amount of syrup.

Meat, kosher or non-kosher, was almost impossible to come by. I would accompany Mutti to the open market, where we would try to buy some fish or chicken. Sometimes she would be able to haggle the price down enough for us to afford it.

Cooking oil was quite expensive so most people used pork lard, which they rendered themselves and used in lieu of the oil. Even though Mutti wasn't able to adhere strictly to all the laws of *kashruth,* she did her best, and she absolutely refused to use any pork products. Instead, she purchased beef fat, which she rendered on our little stove on the roof. We would use this beef fat not only for cooking and frying, but as a spread for bread as well. After a while, we even got used to the taste and tried to imagine it was really chicken fat. It certainly looked like it. When we ran out of oil we used it to light our make-believe candles.

The odor of this fat being rendered was dreadful, and the smell would drift back into the house. I can still remember Dr. Böhm, or Mrs. Ring, calling out to Mutti, "Frau Popielarz, *was sie kochen stinkt ja schrecklich. Bitte machen Sie die Tür zu.*" Closing the rickety roof door didn't help much. Of course Mutti's standard answer would always be, "*Ihr Schweinefett stinkt genau so schlecht.*"

Yet, we were all friends and remained friends—not too easy a proposition, considering the close and oppressive quarters we all shared.

Margarine was not available at all and "*Butterbrot,*" butter, which we had always enjoyed eating on a piece of bread, was mostly unaffordable. There were times, however, when Mutti would be able to purchase about two ounces of the precious commodity. We would use it sparingly to make it last a whole week.

One of the Chinese grocery stores sold second-choice noodles. These were noodles that were swept up from the street after little Chinese boys, chasing the grocery delivery trucks, slit holes in the sacks. They were sold in all shapes and sizes, and were much cheaper than the regular item. In the evening, Mutti and I would sit around the table, and separate the noodles from the pieces of glass, pebbles, rusty nails, and other debris.

The summer months would be the most difficult. We would pass watermelon vendors on the street displaying delicious-looking, mouth-watering pieces of fruit. However, it was not only the flies that were feasting on the watermelon that made it dangerous to eat, but also the fact that it was grown in a diseased swamp. As often as we were tempted, our common sense prevailed. We never touched that fruit during all our years in Shanghai.

When Passover came around, we had a real problem. There were community seders, for which a small fee was charged, but we still needed to buy matzah. By turning in our flour rations to the Jewish Community Center, we were allowed to purchase matzah baked by them in lieu of bread. But it wasn't enough to last the eight days of the festival, for we had no other food to sustain us. As Mutti was servicing a typewriter for one of her yeshiva customers, he happened to mention to her that there was plenty of matzah at his yeshiva. This set Mutti thinking, and she decided to pay the yeshiva a visit. She asked me to accompany her.

A small boy with *payot*, sidelocks, wearing *tzizith*, (fringed undergarment, worn by orthodox Jews), and a yarmulke perched on top of his head, met us at the entrance. In Yiddish, he asked us what we wanted. Mutti told him that she wanted to speak with the Rebbe. He told us to wait, and a few minutes later we were ushered into a fairly large, dimly lighted room.

Behind a long desk, with numerous books piled in front of him, sat an elderly gentleman, with a long beard and glasses perched on the tip of his nose. Actually, he may not have been so elderly, but the beard gave him an "old" appearance. He even reminded me a little of pictures I had seen of my grandfather, Avrohom. If he was surprised by this unexpected visit from a *Yäcke*, a German Jew, he did not show it.

Mutti addressed him deferentially in her German-accented Yiddish. "I understand you may have some extra matzah. I am a widow, my husband died two years ago, and my daughter and I are observant Jews. We do not have enough matzah to tide us over *Pesach*. Would it be possible for you to let us have a few pieces? We would be most appreciative."

"What about the matzoth that were baked in your Community Center. Why don't you get it from them?" he inquired.

"There is simply not enough to go around. We can only buy what is covered by our ration coupons."

"I am sorry, we can't give you any matzah. We need it for our people," he answered, dismissing us with a wave of his hand.

"Wait," Mutti said. She opened her bag and took out a sheaf of papers. "Before we leave, I would like you to read this document. My father wrote this, and I think it will be of interest to you."

The Rebbe, whose name I don't remember, looking puzzled, held his hand out for the papers and started to read. When he finished, he looked at us with new respect.

"Why didn't you tell me right away who you were? I am honored to meet a descendant of an illustrious rabbi as well as one of our great commentators. You can have all the matzah you want, just don't share them with the other *Yäckes!*" he admonished.

After expressing our thanks, we walked out with enough matzah to last the entire festival of Passover.

I was curious. What was in the document, I wanted to know, that made the Rebbe give us all this matzah? Mutti explained that it was Grandfather Avrohom's last will and Testament, written in Hebrew, detailing our genealogy. Avrohom was a descendant of the great Talmudist Akiba Eger, the rabbi-scholar Ezekiel Landau, and the Shach one of the most famous Talmudic commentators.

I had never known that we were descended from "Jewish royalty." This really was exciting!

Chapter 32

Air raid warnings were becoming more frequent. Strafings by American planes became the norm. We had a blackout every night. Trams, cars, and bicycles had their headlights covered with a black filter, and all street lights were out. Even traffic signals were dimmed. We had to use our blackout curtains constantly and were fined if any light was visible through the windows.

If we were in school during an air raid, all classes stopped, and we assembled in one large room. If we should be on a tramway or trolley, we would be allowed to remain on, but it stopped in place as soon as the first siren was heard and did not continue on until the "all clear" was sounded. We never knew at what time we would get home from school. Sometimes the "all clear" sounded within minutes, sometimes we would be stuck on a tram or trolley for hours.

We were advised that the safest place during an air raid, was the ground floor of any building, with doors and windows open. During night air raids, the ten of us would sit huddled in the tiny, damp entranceway waiting for the "all clear." We were also told we could find refuge in the Ward Road jail, which was supposedly bombproof.

Even though the Japanese had strictly forbidden the use of radios during an air raid, we would sometimes switch ours on anyway. If we were lucky, we would be able to hear Radio Chungking, from Chiang Kai-shek's headquarters, also the command post of Major General Claire Chennault who had taken command of the U.S. Fourteenth Air Force in China in 1943. This enabled us to pick up some uncensored war news.

The adults would get excited when they heard that the Americans had either downed an enemy plane or destroyed an enemy vessel. However, the names of the various Pacific islands that were the target of the Americans had very little meaning for us. We had never heard of most of them.

After spending countless nights in the entranceway of our home waiting out an air raid, most of us decided that it wasn't worthwhile staying up. If we were bombed, there wouldn't be much we could do about it anyway. As a matter of fact, day strafings, during school vacations or on weekends, became a game. We would gather on someone's rooftop and watch the American and Japanese fighter planes battle it out in the sky above. We would bet with marbles as to who would shoot down whom. Even though, naturally, we rooted for the Americans and would cheer when the plane with the Red Sun went down in flames, it really didn't matter too much to us. We were in a war zone, and in a very ambiguous situation. Ironically, it was the Japanese who were defending our home, and we were dependent on them for our survival.

Mutti had given me some "emergency" money, which she wanted me to carry in case I was stranded during a long air raid and could not come home for dinner. Even though our repast was meager, nevertheless it was food. One day we were caught in an air raid on Nanking Road on the way home from school. After sitting on the tram for close to two hours, we all got a little bit hungry. I got off the tram with a few friends, and we saw that we had stopped in front of one of the most expensive bakeries in the city. We all started to drool as we looked at the delicious pastries in the window. Finally, one of the girls went in and came out munching on a piece of cake. Some others went in also. The emergency money started to burn a hole in my pocket. Should I? Or shouldn't I?

Finally, my mouth started to water. I went into the bakery and on impulse spent every cent I had—on the biggest piece of cake in the store. We all got back on the tram to eat our goodies. An hour later, the "all clear" sounded, and we were on our way. That's when I started to feel guilty about having spent Mutti's hard-earned money.

When I came home, Mutti was terribly worried. It was later than usual, and though she was aware that there had been an air raid, she didn't know where we had been caught. I told her where we were stopped and then blurted out what I had done.

"You spent all that money on one piece of cake!" she exclaimed. "You had to go into the most expensive bakery in Shanghai. I can't replace that money."

"Don't worry," I replied, very contrite now. "You will save on my dinner. I'm not very hungry and I can have this dinner tomorrow."

Mutti shook her head, then went and told everyone—laughing-ly—how her daughter had picked Shanghai's most expensive bakery to buy a piece of cake. I had a feeling she really wasn't too angry, be-cause she knew how much I had enjoyed it. The following week she gave me "emergency" money again. I swore to her I would be more prudent in the future on how I would spend it.

Actually I was quite thin and, like most of the refugees, suffered from malnutrition. I would break out in chilblains during the winter months. Fingers and toes would take on a bluish hue, and when touched, the area would momentarily turn white.

When we lived in the French Concession, the exterminators were able to control some of the bugs, like the large spiders, lice, cen-tipedes and cockroaches, even the rats, though they never got rid of them entirely. However, in the ghetto, there was no way to control the vermin, even with the Flit.

After seeing a few mice running around, I got myself a tiger-striped cat, appropriately named Tiger, who very proudly presented us with a mouse's tail a few times a week. I missed Duke whom I had left behind with Zyama Lifschitz when we had to move to the ghetto.

Head lice had also settled in my hair, as they did in that of my schoolmates'; and we had to shampoo with kerosene regularly. Then, of course, everyone had to contend with intestinal worms. We would unknowingly consume the eggs with some of our food, or they would enter our system via the air we breathed. We only became aware that they were breeding in our intestines when a weight loss was ex-perienced, or when they were excreted.

The tapeworm was much more dangerous, for it would be ex-creted in pieces and we never knew when the medicine taken to con-trol it was effective. Mutti and I both suffered from these worms, on and off, and we had to take this medication almost constantly. This condition, coupled with the malnutrition, contributed to our weight loss and low resistance to disease.

Starving Chinese and corpses on sidewalks had been a common sight in Shanghai since our arrival, but now we began to see emaciated and starving people among the refugees. One day we en-countered a man, who must have been quite handsome at one time, filthy, with matted blond hair, clad in rags and covered with all kinds of sores. I realized he was one of the refugees.

"Who is that?" I asked Mutti.

"That," replied Mutti sadly, "was a very renowned judge in Germany. It seems he cannot cope with the conditions here."

A week later we heard that this former judge had died of starvation. There were many others like him.

When the typhoon season came around in the fall, it was much worse in Hongkew than in other parts of the city. The sewage system backed up. Streets were flooded, and we all wore high boots to walk around. The only means of transportation was the rickshaw. The coolie would roll up his trousers and wade through the dirty water. The floods were unhealthy, but they did not bother us kids. We made a game of wading through the streets, and besides, school would usually be closed till the floods subsided.

September 30, 1943, was going to be our first *Rosh Hashanah,* the Jewish New Year, in the ghetto. The little *shul* on Ward Road could not accommodate the many refugees who wanted to attend High Holiday services. The only suitable locations were the two Chinese movie theaters situated just outside the ghetto limits. The Jüdische Gemeinde petitioned the Japanese authorities for permission to conduct services at these two locations. Permission was granted, and these two theaters were rented for *Rosh Hashanah* and *Yom Kippur.*

Anyone who wanted to attend had to purchase a ticket, which permitted them to exit the ghetto to attend these services. The women sat upstairs in the balcony, and the men were seated below. The stage served as the *bimah* from which services were conducted, and Torahs were borrowed from synagogues outside the ghetto. When services ended, the Chinese customers were waiting impatiently outside for their movies to start, yet they would yell out to us, as we passed, "*Kung tchie fahseh* (Happy New Year)."

To my knowledge, no one ever used the synagogue entrance ticket as a subterfuge for leaving the ghetto to go elsewhere, which would undoubtedly have jeopardized the rest of us.

Our situation seemed to become more and more hopeless. Mutti and I had decided never to sell Vati's gold watch. It would be our memento of him. However, Mutti sold her own gold watch, and then reluctantly, mine—the one Omi had given me. A little while later, she sold one of the gold bars on the black market and was doing everything possible to hold on to the other two.

And then we saw "the light at the end of the tunnel."

The U.S. Government was well aware of the plight of the refugees in Shanghai. After all, the Joint was relentlessly pressuring them for permission to transmit funds to the ghetto community. However, it was not till the beginning of 1944 that this permission was granted. By that time, Laura Margulies, now back in New York, had given her report. And there was pressure from well-known Jewish leaders too. President Roosevelt had been informed of the Nazi atrocities in Europe, and this information too may have influenced the government's position concerning us. In any case, whatever the reason for the change in policy, funds were received and administered by the Jüdische Gemeinde. Even though our lot had improved—starvation was not imminent—conditions were still miserable. But there was hope that we would at least survive.

Mutti and I took advantage of the soup kitchen only occasionally—when we were hungry enough to be desperate. Otherwise, we still preferred eating alone.

Chapter 33

Through the grapevine, we heard about the Normandy invasion on June 6, 1944 (June 7 in the Pacific). Though it did not directly affect us, it set us to wondering anew what was happening to our friends and relatives left behind in Europe.

Joseph, was he still at the Veterans Hospital in Breslau? Or the Kiewes—did Ruth make it to Palestine? What about Leo in France— where was he now? Was Samuel and his family still in Berlin? Were they being bombed? And what about Henoch and his wife in Frankfurt and the rest of our relatives in Kalisz— how were they faring? We had absolutely no inkling as to what was going on in that part of Europe.

Life went on as well as can be expected under abnormal conditions. People were still getting married and babies were born, and the cemeteries were filling up. There were even a few intermarriages between refugees and Orientals.

It was extremely difficult for a young married couple to get started, for there was no place to live. Most of the time, they would share a room with the parents of one of them, the sleeping quarters separated by a curtain. The parents would take discreet walks or go visiting in the evening, in order to give the newlyweds some semblance of privacy.

The refugee community itself lived in a curious *Catch 22* dilemma. We were hated as the despised *Na'aku'ning* (foreigners), by the Chinese, who still looked upon us as representatives of the colonial interlopers. The Nazi Fifth Column, firmly entrenched in Shanghai as allies of the Japanese, considered us, of course, *"dreckige Juden,"* who had eluded their extermination machine. And, to the Japanese, who were not anti-Semitic, we were simply enemies of their allies. We hadn't done anything to anybody, but somehow we had become everybody's scapegoat.

It was not unusual for us to be physically harassed by Chinese youths while walking in the ghetto streets. We learned, especially the girls, always to walk in groups. Chinese teenagers frequently tried to jostle us or threw rocks, or pushed us into the gutter.

One day, while I was walking with one of my friends, a group of Chinese youths started pushing us around. We got very frightened. It was almost dark, and there was no policeman in sight. We started to run, and they ran after us throwing rocks. Out of nowhere, a Japanese soldier materialized. He pointed his gun at the youths and collared the ringleader while the rest ran away. Then, he took the butt of his gun and beat the boy till he lay bleeding on the sidewalk. We stood cowering against a wall.

"You all right?" he asked gruffly.

We nodded numbly. "Yes, we are. *Arregato. Kam ban wa.* (Thank you, good evening.)"

The Japanese did their best to protect us from hoodlums. They were not too fond of the Chinese—as their record in their long war against China horrifyingly shows.

Chapter 34

April 13, 1945.

The radio blasted the news in six languages, and the newspapers screamed their headlines: Our great hero (because that is what we thought of him then), President Franklin Delano Roosevelt, had died. Harry Truman, a man unknown to us, was now President of the United States. We conducted a memorial service and recited *Kaddish* in the little ghetto shul.

But on the heels of that came the best of all possible news: the capitulation of Nazi Germany. And with it lamentations of our particular plight:

"You see, I told you we should have stayed home and taken our chances. Now the war is over in Europe, and we're still here."

"It would have been better in a concentration camp. At least we would have had food and wouldn't have had to endure this horrible climate."

"Europe would have been much safer for us."

The chorus went on and on. Husbands to wives, wives to husbands. Recriminations for having left Europe and come to "this godforsaken place."

Via the Red Cross, we now tried to get word about friends and relatives left behind in Europe. And that's when the real horror started—the grim, incomprehensible news. In dribs and drabs, we heard about the extermination camps. . . gas chambers. . . medical experiments. . . women and little children dead—thousands, no, tens of thousands, no, hundreds of thousands, millions. How many million?

We could not believe it. It must be Japanese propaganda—they just want to scare us. It must be because the war isn't going well for them either. We were still in a war zone. What was going to happen to us now? We were the forgotten people. No one would even know where we are or even care. Was there anyone *left* to care?

Individual Red Cross inquiries got us nowhere. They had no

answers. They took the information and promised they would keep us informed.

Life had now taken on a new meaning for us. The little we had heard about the conditions in Europe, the death camps, the unbelievable massacres, brought all of us closer together. Everyone had left someone dear behind—many someones. Even though we had no details, memorial services were held. Lists of relatives and friends in Europe were compiled. The refugee community was in shock.

No more recriminations. Shanghai was indeed our haven.

"Actually the heat isn't so bad if we don't venture out between noon and two in the afternoon."

"If we drink a lot of water, we probably won't be so hungry."

"Ghoya does give us passes. So what if he slapped some people around a little bit? But he never killed anyone."

"The Japanese really are not anti-Semitic, and now the Germans have surrendered, they're not being pressured anymore to discriminate against us."

Thus went the comments. But we still worried. When would it be over for us? Where were the Americans? Till now the city itself had not been bombed. We had been strafed, but only the outskirts had been bombed.

July 17, 1945, seemed like any other day. It was the height of the summer, and the heat and humidity were oppressive, as usual. Mutti had left the city on her almost daily rounds of the Chinese shops. She had just sold her second gold bar on the black market, and was going to buy as much merchandise as possible, for her pink pass was expiring this week, and Okura, who was now handling the pink passes, had told her that he was issuing her last renewal—the few typewriter customers she serviced did not warrant her trips to the city, therefore she was no longer eligible to receive a pass. I had already helped her compose a letter, in English, to Okura, pleading with him to give her at least one more renewal.

Because my own pass was valid only during the school year, I could not even go to the city with her. I saw that we were out of boiled drinking water, but I did not have enough money to buy boiled water. I had to be satisfied with hot water, which I had poured into a large pot and set on our little roof stove.

I fanned the coals, trying to bring it to a boil, but it seemed to take forever. When it finally bubbled, I let it boil another five minutes, then placed the pot in some cold water in the sink, which was running for a change, and after it cooled down a bit, I poured it into bottles, which I placed in the icebox. This week Mutti had been able to afford a small block of ice. Even though the Chinese only drank hot water because it was supposed to be healthier, I hated it. I liked it cold.

Having completed this hateful but necessary chore, and exhausted from the heat and the fanning of the stove, I decided to take a walk to the other end of the ghetto, to the SACRA buildings where my friends Susie and Chaya lived. Chaya's mother always saved me a piece of gefilte fish, and I was hungry.

I started to walk along Ward Road and on my way I passed the jail, where I stopped as usual in front of the balconies of the jail hospital. Wounded American POWs were housed there and sometimes would be allowed out on the balcony. We waved to them whenever we went by, and they waved back. I am sure they had no idea that they were waving at refugees who were not much better off than they were.

That day, there were about five POWs on one of the upper balconies. I waved to them, they waved back, and then began clapping their hands and throwing kisses. One of them performed a little pirouette. I looked quickly around to see if any Japanese soldiers were watching this forbidden display, but the only people I saw were some other refugees, who had also stopped to wave to the soldiers.

It was then that the sirens went off. People started running toward the jail to take refuge. The sirens kept wailing, on and on and on. I didn't know what to do. It was frightening, for this sequence was the dreaded signal, the one we hoped never to hear, warning us that Shanghai was under attack. The sky was overcast, the air still and very humid. I heard the planes, but couldn't see them.

I had to make a fast decision: Go to the jail, continue on to

SACRA, or get back home quickly and sit near the door. The decision was made for me. I heard a long whistle and then bombs started to fall. Explosion after explosion. I ducked into one of the little curbside trenches. I heard people running, screaming, shouting, a babble of tongues. I tried to understand what people were saying.

And then I heard in German: "We're under attack. The Americans are bombing the ghetto. Everyone stay where you are."

I didn't dare move. Two Chinese women were huddled in the little trench with me, wailing incessantly. I tried to cover my ears. I could hear the airplanes, the whistle of descending bombs, just before they exploded, and the sirens were still ringing and ringing, a sound that bothers me to this day.

Where was Mutti? I wanted my mother. I didn't want to die alone, killed by an American bomb. Time seemed to stand still till the "all clear" sounded. I crawled out of my little hole, and there was dead silence, nothing seemed disturbed. Then someone said, "they got the radio station at Point Road, and there are thousands dead."

People were running all over the place. Those who had taken refuge in the Ward Road jail ran out to see the damage. People were screaming, we saw Japanese soldiers trying to control the crowds, clearing traffic to let the ambulances and fire brigade through.

I ran home to wait for Mutti. It seemed like an eternity till she arrived. She had been on a tramway near The Bund during the bombardment, where she waited it out. Her heart had stopped when she could see over the Garden Bridge that Hongkew was under attack, and she knew that I was at home. Neither of us knew whether we'd ever see each other again.

That evening, we went to one of the little refugee coffeehouses on Chusan Road to celebrate our good luck in having survived the bombardment. On the Sabbath, we were going to go to the synagogue to *bensh gomel*, a special prayer recited after one has survived a catastrophe. That's when we heard the sad news that about thirty refugees had been killed during the attack and many hundreds wounded. Also thousands of Chinese had been killed.

The Japanese rescue squads had done their job well. The ambulances were there immediately to take care of the casualties, and they had delivered supplies and equipment to the refugee hospital to take care of the wounded. Mutti and I later went to the hospitals, for among the casualties were some of her friends, and I discovered that Chaya had also been wounded—luckily not severely, just shrapnel wounds on her back that would heal in time but leave scars.

Suddenly it hit me. If I hadn't stopped those extra few minutes to wave to the American POWs, I would have been in the midst of the bombardments, for I was en route to Chaya's house when the raid started.

Now we were truly frightened. When would the Americans return with their bombs? They had inflicted only slight damage. Were they trying to destroy Shanghai? After all, it was a port and therefore militarily strategic to the Japanese. We had survived so long, would it all end now? Would we ever live to see the end of the war? We would have to take the air raids more seriously.

On August 6, 1945, a terrible rumor started. The Americans had dropped a new kind of bomb on Hiroshima, a Japanese city. It was not announced on the radio. All we heard through the grapevine was that the bomb was so dreadful it had totally destroyed that city. Then a few days later, on August 9, we heard that another such bomb was dropped on Nagasaki, another Japanese city. It too was totally destroyed. Were the Americans going to drop this dreadful bomb on Shanghai too?

Some people thought that these bombardments signaled the end of the war in the Pacific and were arranging celebrations. American and British flags were displayed. The Japanese quickly pulled them down and threatened to proclaim a total curfew if these flags were displayed again.

August 17 was again a very hot day. The sun was shining brightly. We hadn't had any air raids for over a week now. Everything seemed calm. I was on the grounds of the Kadoorie School when we heard the distinct motor of airplanes. Curiously, there were no sirens this time. Then we saw a huge grey plane with a little white star on its wing swoop low. We knew it was not a Japanese plane because it did not have the Rising Sun on it. It couldn't be American, not flying so low without being attacked. What kind of plane was it? Russian, perhaps, because of the star, even though it was white and not red.

Then, as we looked up, we were showered with hundreds of leaflets, and we were forced to realize that it was an American plane, after all. The leaflets were in English, advising us to stay put, not to engage in any demonstrations, and to go about our business as usual. No sirens, no bombs, no Japanese interceptor planes—also no one stopping us from collecting the leaflets. Allied victory *must* be in sight!

We wondered why the Americans chose to drop these leaflets into the ghetto. Who did they think we were? Only a month ago they'd been bombing us.

We were a little cautious with our celebrations. However, some of the refugees took it upon themselves to beat up several Japanese officials from Ghoya's office, as well as some of the refugees who had worked there. Ghoya and Okura themselves had quietly disappeared. It was not till five days later, August 22, that Ghoya's pass office was officially closed. However, the ghetto was still in existence, with the Russian and Sikh guards stationed at the entrance and exit.

When will the Americans, our liberators, arrive, we wondered. Twelve days later, on September 3, Maj. Gen. Claire Chennault of the U.S. Fourteenth Air Force and General Chiang Kai-shek arrived in Shanghai to repossess the city for the Chinese Republic. This dreadful war was over for us too. Now, we could finally celebrate V-J-Day.

PART IV

Liberation
1945–1947

VOLUME : 1　　　　　　　　　　　　　　　　　　　**ISSUE : 2**

DID SO — MANY OWE

NEVER BEFORE IN HISTORY

SO MUCH TO SO FEW (CHURCHILL)

MAJOR GENERAL CLAIRE L. CHENNAULT

PUBLISHED BY THE SHANGHAI JEWISH YOJTH COMMUNITY CENTER

Liberation issue of *FUTURE*, our youth ghetto magazine, featuring
Major General Claire Chennault.

Chapter 35

The ghetto had finally been opened just before the first Americans came in, and we all went wild. I remember it well. Somehow everyone had congregated in the little *shul* on Ward Road. Word had gone out that a Jewish American soldier was there. I had never seen an American soldier. Yet there he was, young and handsome in his uniform, surrounded by a crowd. Then we found out that he was the son of one of the refugee families. They had sent him to England in 1938 on one of the children transports. He had enlisted in the RAF and then went to America, where he enlisted in the Army Air Corps. Somehow he had gotten word that his parents were in the Shanghai ghetto, and there was an emotional reunion after seven long years of separation.

V–J Day parties were arranged everywhere, and a parade on Nanking Road was scheduled to include all the "enemy aliens" who were interned during the war and were now being repatriated to their respective countries.

I missed it all. I was sick in bed with jaundice and had to be on a strict diet. How Mutti did it, I will never know, but she managed to get me lean meat, cooked in water with a boiled tomato, almost every day.

My friends came to console me. Don't worry about not being out in the streets, they said. School was still closed, because we were getting our building back, and it had to be renovated. Also, the city was in chaos. There was no one in charge.

Chiang Kai-shek's control of the city was very loose—the hoodlums were running wild in the streets, attacking foreigners as never before. In addition, the U.S. Navy had just entered port, and no young female was safe in the streets. Word was out that the sailors were raping anything that moved, they had been at sea for a very long time.

I recovered just when classes resumed in our old school building. The Japanese had left it in pretty good shape. It had withstood the war well, and was never used as a hospital. However, none of our former teachers returned. Mrs. Hekking went back to the Netherlands, and our British teachers returned home to England.

Our new headmaster was a Mr. Holland. He had just arrived from England and stood ramrod straight in his six foot six inches. He was extremely strict, and I never saw him crack a smile. Discipline, which had been rather loose while we were at the Shanghai Jewish Club, was now stricter than ever. We did not have to study Japanese any longer, but Chinese was added to our curriculum. We sang "God Save the King" again as well as "*Hatikvah.*"

The new administration arranged free transportation to the school out of Hongkew, on a truck that picked us up at a gathering point in the morning and brought us back after classes. It was an open truck, with minimal seating on benches that were attached on each side.

Once these seats were taken, we either sat on the floor or on the back of the truck with our feet dangling. These were the choice seats. A tarpaulin sheltered us during inclement weather.

Sometimes, we would hitchhike home. The American soldiers were very casual about letting us ride on their trucks, weapon carriers, or jeeps. I am sure it was against regulations, but with the liberation forces, there seemed to be a laissez-faire kind of attitude. Usually when a soldier gave us a ride, he would also give us some chocolate and chewing gum. This in itself was worth the ride. It was also much more comfortable than our school truck.

One day, our truck broke down at the corner near the hotel where many American officers were being housed. As we waited for repairs, we saw large, sausage-shaped balloons floating down, at which the boys laughed hysterically. We could not understand what was so funny. Finally, one of the boys condescended to tell us that the "balloons" were really blown-up condoms. Undoubtedly the soldiers thought it was a great joke.

We again had our regular sports activities—hockey, track, football, volleyball, and badminton. I still played center field hockey and became captain of our team.

Efforts were being made by the refugees to leave Shanghai as quickly as possible—not only because we had never considered the city as our permanent home but also because we realized there would soon be a Communist takeover. We certainly did not want to be caught in another war, a civil war this time. But where were we going to go? Everyone wrote to contacts in Palestine, England, Australia, and the United States.

We were hoping that the war would have eased the immigration laws of the various countries. But not much had changed. The world still did not open its doors to newcomers too quickly.

Palestine, still under the British Mandate, did not allow for mass immigration of Jews, for the British still wanted to pacify the Arabs.

England was recovering from a war that had not only ruined her economy but also her cities. She was in dire assistance, some of which she got from the United States, but she couldn't take immigrants. She was accepting only her own subjects, who returned home from various places of internment throughout Asia.

Australia was allowing some refugees to apply for immigration, but it was going to take awhile, and only young people were initially accepted. Later, they could apply to have their parents join them.

The United States still had her quota system, which was being applied a little more liberally. If an affidavit could be obtained, the visa would be issued under Displaced Persons status.

Because Mutti and I qualified under the German Displaced Persons quota, I wrote to my great-aunt Rose, in Brooklyn, asking her again to sponsor us, explaining that Omi and Vati had died in Shanghai, so that she would only have to send papers for the two of us. Her daughter, a teacher, whose husband was a high school principal in Brooklyn, replied that her mother had died during the war. She explained that she was very sorry, but their salaries could not support the two of us.

I wrote again and told them that I was fifteen years old, fluent in English, and would be able to work and support Mutti and myself, and that Mutti could work also, and we would not be a burden to anyone. She replied again, sorry, they can't sponsor us.

Mutti then wrote to Moritz to see if perhaps we could come to England. Apparently not, but Aunt Henny advised us that she would contact a niece who had emigrated to the United States before the war. She had married there and was now living in Lakewood, New Jersey, and perhaps she would be willing to sponsor us.

In the summer of 1946 we received a letter from Edith and Max Heinrich, saying that they would be happy to sponsor us!

We were overjoyed. Finally, we would be going to America. We could hardly believe it. We obtained all the immigration forms from the American Consulate and sent them on to Lakewood posthaste.

It would take time, we were warned, but this time we did not worry. We had waited so long, what would a few more years matter?

Many people started receiving affidavits from the United States and immigration papers from Australia, and now the problem was transport. When would ships become available for the refugee passengers, for all the available space was needed to bring the troops home.

Chapter 36

Right on the heels of the Americans came another welcome relief, the United Nations Relief and Rehabilitation Association (UNRRA), and they brought food. The Far Eastern Office of the Joint administered the food distribution, which consisted of American army K-rations.

We received our allotment coupons and now queued up happily and willingly to get decent food. Everything, of course, was in tins. Pudding, butter, cheese, desserts, eggs, bread, cake, meat, fish, as well as all kinds of snacks. We also received the "jungle" chocolate, one piece of which had enough nutrients to sustain a soldier who might be in the jungle for days, or even weeks, and now it was going to sustain us. Mutti exchanged her bacon tins for tunafish. We had not seen so much food in years—we had K-ration parties, where everyone would bring a different product from his ration kit, which we pooled.

Hongkew could not be called a ghetto any longer—we could come and go as we pleased. Still, no one moved out of their "ghetto" quarters. In hopes that we would be departing Shanghai in the near future, it did not pay to relocate again.

Mutti was hoping to reestablish her typewriter business as soon as the American, British, and other foreign firms reopened their offices. In the meantime, she was hired as a typewriter mechanic by the U.S. Army Quartermaster General's office, earning a comparatively good salary.

The Joint, now firmly entrenched again in Shanghai, sent over various staff members to facilitate our emigration. They helped us write letters, acted as a liaison with the various consulates, and paid for steamship tickets for those fortunate enough to receive a visa.

Then Charles Jordan arrived. He was on the Joint staff in the United States and was sent by them to Shanghai to help the Jewish refugee youth. He established a Jewish Youth Community Center at the Kadoorie School in Hongkew. He familiarized us with life in the United States and the job, business, and educational opportunities we could look forward to. He encouraged all of us in whatever we wanted to do in our hopes for the future. He became our mentor, friend, confidant. He was a morale booster and gave us strength and hope for a new life. Anyone who was ever touched by Charlie Jordan has never forgotten him.

(He later headed the Paris office of the Joint, where I visited with him in 1953. In 1956 he went to Czechoslovakia to assist the Jewish community, who had a hard time coping under the Communist regime. Possibly he assisted them too well for the regime to tolerate; a short time later, his body was found floating in the Danube.)

XMHA was our favorite radio station, particularly because it was the U.S. Army station. We listened to American music, Frank Sinatra was the big rage—and "The Shadow." We heard bubble gum and chewing gum commercials (probably the only people who actually enjoyed the commercials), and listened to jitterbug and lindy music.

My friends and I took dancing lessons. We had been brought up on the waltz and the tango, so the fast tempo of the popular American music was just right for us teenagers. And anyway we were bound to gobble up everything American.

Our big recreation was to go to the docks to meet the sailors. It was all in fun. Most of the time I would go with Susie. We would look for the hospital ship *Hope,* and usually some kind sailor would see us and either smuggle us aboard to watch a movie and give us a meal, or come down and give us some chocolate, chewing gum, or silk stockings.

One day I met a young sailor from Milwaukee. He had never met a Jew before, but was willing to sponsor Mutti and me to come to the United States, in case the affidavit from the Heinrichs would not be accepted. I know Mutti would have had a fit if she had suspected that I had even talked to a sailor—that was a big "no-no" in Europe. but he was a nice boy. He used to bring me food from the ship and wrote to me from Milwaukee after his discharge.

While waiting for our papers, I realized that I would have to look for a job as soon as we arrived in the United States. I was sixteen years old. I had always known how to type, because I grew up with typewriters. I borrowed a typing book and a Gregg shorthand book and taught myself touch typing and shorthand.

Finally, our papers arrived from Lakewood. We were summoned

to the American Consulate and interviewed by the vice consul. As we walked into his office, he glanced up from the papers he was studying.

"You are Rika and Evelyn P-p-popp," he stammered, being unable to pronounce our name. he finally gave up and spelled it: "Er—P-O-P-I-E-L-A-R-Z." He handed us some papers. "Here are your visas for the United States. You can leave whenever you are ready. Good luck!" he said, smiling, and that's all there was to it.

The date was January 29, 1947. Had Vati lived, this would have been my parents' eighteenth wedding anniversary. The number 18 in Hebrew stands for *chai*, life, and we were going to a new life, in a new country, after a wait of twelve long years, much suffering, deprivation, and tragedy, from the time of our first application to the United States. It also had been Vati's dream.

I was in my last semester of school, in Form VI Upper. Should we wait till the end of the term in June or leave on the first available ship? Once before, in 1933, we had waited and paid dearly. Could it happen again? We were afraid. When would the Communist takeover take place? It would be better if we sacrificed my graduation, which could always be made up, and leave as soon as space was available.

It came sooner than expected. The Joint purchased steamship tickets for us on the SS *General Gordon*, of the American President Lines, departing Shanghai March 6.

1947 graduating class of the Shanghai Jewish School.
Front row: second from left—Ellen Salomon; directly behind her—
Ethel Shmulewitz. Seated, on right: the author—next to her: Susie Kushner
Lipsey. Directly behind her: Chaya Ambaras.

Chapter 37

We were saying good-bye all over again. But now it was different. Some of my friends had already departed, either for America or for Australia, and some were going on the same ship as us. Still others were waiting to get into Palestine. No one was returning to Europe. There were farewell parties almost every day.

Mutti exchanged her last gold bar for American dollars. We had to buy suitcases and some decent clothes. We sold our furniture to the Chinese living in our lane, but packed whatever was still left of our German possessions. Mutti, luckily, had been able to hold on to some of our monogrammed, silver-plated flatware, which had been her engagement gift, the silver-plated *kiddush* cup and *etrog* box that had belonged to grandfather Avrohom, as well as the gorgeous antique-brass *Hanukkah* menorah and candlesticks. (*Etrog* is a citron imported from Israel, used during the festival of *Sukkoth*.)

The most difficult farewell took place at the cemeteries. We were leaving Vati and Omi in their graves in a strange land. We

Father's grave, Columbia Road cemetery, Shanghai. The two hands signify that he was a *Cohen*, descended from the High Priest in the Temple at Jerusalem.

Note: Sadly, the cemetery is no longer in existence. During China's "Cultural Revolution," this cemetery and others were razed for the construction of new buildings.

took photographs of their graves. We knew we would probably never return, and no one would ever visit them. What was going to become of the cemeteries once the Communists took over, we wondered.

(A few years ago, when researching the fate of the refugee cemeteries in Shanghai, I discovered that during the Cultural Revolution, the Communists razed the stones and built housing developments over them.)

Our ship had not as yet been reconverted from a troop transport into a normal passenger ship. Consequently, our accommodations were arranged dormitory style: men and women in separate quarters, older people in the lower bunks while the upper bunks were for the younger set. The toilets and dining room were communal. The food was pretty dreadful, and the crew did not seem too happy with us either, but we didn't complain. Who cared? We were leaving the Orient for good. We were going to America.

Just before docking in Hawaii, we ran into a storm, and the ship received an S.O.S. from an LST that was going under. We had to change course and pick up survivors, who were bobbing around in rubber life rafts. We all helped bring them aboard and tended to their injuries, and then dropped them off in Hawaii. It gave all of us a great feeling of satisfaction that, in a small way, we had been able to help save the lives of some American servicemen. We even speculated that these same men may have had a hand in ending the war which brought us our liberation.

We were not allowed off in Hawaii—our first glimpse of paradise. Instead we sailed on to San Francisco. On Thursday morning, March 20, we passed under the Golden Gate Bridge. It was an unforgettable morning, windy and crisp, but the sun was shining. We were all out on deck waiting for our first glimpse of America, and threw some of our Chinese coins into the water. Everyone cheered, and then we cried, we could hardly believe we were here at last.

And then we cried again for all those who didn't make it. For our countless relatives and friends who had ended up in Hitler's ovens. Mutti and I cried for Omi who had made it to Shanghai, where she had died of a broken heart. But most of all we cried for Vati, who was always so full of life, who had played so many enjoyable games with me, who had always laughed and told jokes, and in the end was so terribly betrayed by the country he had loved so much and had been ready to sacrifice his life for. In return for his devotion, that same country sent him to Buchenwald and finally to a lonely grave in Shanghai.

Mutti and I took some slight solace from the fact that Vati and Omi had at least not perished in the gas chambers.

PART V

A Dream Come True
1947–1951

Republic of China)
Province of Kiangsu)
City of Shanghai) SS:
Consulate General of the)
United States of America)

Before me, John H. Stutesman, Jr. Vice Consul of the United States of America in and for the Consular district of Shanghai, China, duly commissioned and qualified, personally appeared **Evelyn Popielarz** who, being duly sworn, deposes and says:

That ~~his~~ (her) name is Evelyn POPIELARZ and ~~the~~ (she) resides at 498/8 Ward Road, Shanghai, China

that ~~he~~ (she) was born at Breslau, Germany on July 31, 1930.

That ~~he~~ (she) is at present unable to obtain a passport as ~~xxxxxxxxxxxxxxxxxxxxxxxxxxxxx~~ ~~xxxxxxxxxxxxxxxxxxxxxxxxxxxxxxxxxxxxx~~ ~~Unitxxxxxxxxxxxxx~~ she is stateless.

That a signed photograph of the affiant partially impressed by the consular seal of the American Consulate General, Shanghai, China is attached below;

That ~~he~~ (she) makes this affidavit to serve in lieu of a passport to proceed to the United States;

AND further deponent saith not.

Evelyn Popielarz

Subscribed and sworn to before me this 29th day of January 1947. ~~19__~~

John H. Stutesman, Jr.
John H. Stutesman, Jr.
American Vice Consul

DESCRIPTION OF AFFIANT

Height: 5' 1"
Color of hair: brown
Color of eyes: blue
Distinguished marks: - - -

Place and date of birth:
Breslau, Germany, July 31, 1930.
Occupation:
Student.

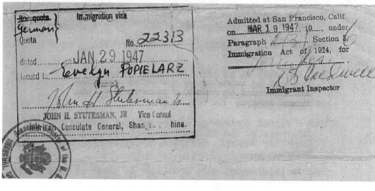

Front: Author's U.S. visa application.
Back: Visa—date of January 29 was date of parents' wedding.

Chapter 38

When we docked in San Francisco, Joint volunteers boarded the ship with cups of coffee and snacks. That was fortunate, for the crew had left the ship, and there was no heat or food. Customs and Immigration took all day, the last passengers not debarking until midnight.

Two volunteer families, the Gruens and the Lunds, "adopted" us. They put us in a taxi, which took us to the Filmore Hotel on Filmore Street. This was the first time in many years that I had seen a plastered ceiling, not just one with beams and spaces. But the real luxury was having a private bath and toilet again, no mosquitos, cockroaches, or rats.

The following day we were allowed to pick out clothing that had been donated by Jewish families in San Francisco. I was thrilled to be able to wear some modern American clothes, for even though they were not new, they were in good condition, had been cleaned, and were still in style.

The Gruens had fled from Germany in 1938, as had Harry Lund. Libby Lund had come from a farm in Iowa (her Polish-born grandmother had settled there in 1880) and still retained her distinctive Midwestern accent. They took turns in having us dine with them in their homes during our stay in San Francisco.

As I had come to Shanghai at the tender age of eight, I grew up to believe that water can only be drunk after having been boiled and that raw fruits and vegetables were taboo. Now, all of a sudden, I could drink water from the tap, eat all kinds of delicious fruit after just washing it under the tap, and have meat for dinner.

I had known drugstores only as pharmacies, where you purchased medicine. Here, a drugstore had a counter at which I could sit and drink a coke, a milkshake or an ice cream soda—an American institution, that was very exciting to a young teenager, particularly one who had been deprived for so long.

The Joint was in charge of resettling all the arriving refugees within the United States. We were free to go wherever we chose. At first, Mutti and I contemplated staying in San Francisco. However, New York had always been the glamour capital which I had wanted to see. It would also be proper for us to meet the people who had sponsored us, and Lakewood, New Jersey was not too far from New York City. Before we made a final decision, we wanted to see New York.

After about a week in San Francisco, the Joint put us on a Pullman to New York, from which we took a bus to Lakewood. We were most warmly and affectionately welcomed by the Heinrichs and their little children, and got our first taste of American small-town life. The Heinrichs were Orthodox, and it was a pleasure to be able to eat kosher food again.

They were incredibly kind and hospitable, but we did not want to be a burden to them, and after a few weeks in their home, we decided to make our own way. Right after the war, Mutti had tried to find out what had happened to our friends the Kiewes, the family friends I had stayed with during the *Kristallnacht* rampage in 1938. We discovered that Mrs. Kiewe and her mother had perished in the gas chambers, but Ruth had gone on to Palestine and right after the war had emigrated to New York, where she had an uncle and various cousins.

We contacted her from Lakewood and arranged to meet in New York. After a very emotional reunion at Grand Central Station, we proceeded to her uncle's apartment on Park Avenue. He had generously given us permission to stay there during our visit while he was away on vacation. And what an apartment it was! Marble baths, sculptured rugs, velvet curtains. Just like the movies, we thought. (Ruth, who had never married, now lives in Chicago. We speak to each other regularly.)

The decision was made to make New York our home. We contacted NYANA, the New York Association for New Americans, an arm of the Joint, who put us up at a hotel and then found a furnished room for us on Amsterdam Avenue.

Americans still found it difficult to pronounce our name and it bothered Mutti terribly to hear it butchered by mispronunciation. She decided to Americanize it to *Portan.*

Chapter 39

New York

It was a shock to run into a new kind of prejudice, one I had never come across before—the hatred that American Jews of Eastern European origin bore for German Jews.

Our landlady, Mrs. Malinow, was in her late sixties or early seventies. She was born in Russia and had come to the United States as a young girl, where she married and was now widowed. Mutti communicated with her in Yiddish. Her married daughter lived in the area, she said. More from loneliness than from need for funds, she had decided to rent out one of her rooms and had registered with NYANA.

Even though the room was small and dreary, overlooking a narrow courtyard, it was clean, and Mrs. Malinow seemed a kindly old lady. She would allow us to boil water for coffee or tea in her kitchen, and would take messages for us on her telephone till we could afford our own. We would pay for any outside calls.

Everything seemed pleasant enough the first few days. Then we met her daughter. The minute she heard that we were from Germany, she started screaming at us that German Jews were the vilest creatures on earth, that they came to New York in the thirties with their fine furniture and went into business, while Americans, especially American Jews, were starving. Hitler was probably right, she ranted, and they deserved what they got.

I stared, dumbfounded. A Jew saying that about other Jews— Jewish anti-Semitism? I stood there in shock, while Mutti went white with rage, and Mrs. Malinow bit her lip in shame. "I will talk to you later," she said to Mutti, pushing her daughter into the living room.

Mutti quickly soothed me and said we'd find another place to live. Mrs. Malinow came out of her room, crying, apologizing for her daughter's behavior, and begging us not to move. However, she did agree—as her daughter demanded—that we should no longer have the use of her stove or the telephone.

Mutti tried to explain to me this terrible antipathy between Eastern European Jew and German Jew.

It seems that at the turn of the century, when German Jews were pretty well educated and assimilated into German society (much like today's American Jews), their Eastern European brethren were still being hunted by Cossacks in the Ukraine and Poland. Savage pogroms took place in many of the *shtetls* and cities.

To escape these horrors, many Jews fled across the border into Germany. They were destitute, and German Jews were only too happy to give them money, food, and clothing. However, they were not so willing to accept them in their homes and socialize with them. These *Ostjuden*, Eastern Jews, spoke Yiddish—at the time considered a butchered, ungrammatical German— and dressed in the ways of the *shtetl*. The women wore *sheitels* and long dresses with long sleeves, while the men sported *payot*, and their clothing consisted of the black caftan plus black hat or fur *streiml*. In short, they looked rather like modern Hasidim, and the sophisticated German Jews disclaimed them, as many of today's assimilated American Jews distance themselves from American Hasidim.

It was all ludicrous yet chilling. Why couldn't people be tolerant of differences. Isn't that what brought on Hitler and the war?

A few days after this incident, as Mutti and I approached the apartment house, a young man followed us into the lobby. Somehow, he made us feel uneasy. Mutti whispered to me in German to watch out and get into the apartment very quickly. Just as she unlocked the door, he tried to push his way in. We managed to slam the door on him just in time and fasten the chain.

We called to Mrs. Malinow and then realized that she wasn't home. In the meantime, the stranger kept banging on the door, trying to push it in. We got worried on two counts. Should Mrs. Malinow come home this minute, he would encounter her, and who knows what would happen? If she didn't come home, we were virtual prisoners in the apartment.

We tried to pry open the door where the phone was locked up, but to no avail. I then hit upon the idea of opening a window and attracting someone's attention on the other side of the courtyard. After a few minutes of shouting and waving, I managed to tell the occupant across the way that the police should be called. Shortly thereafter, our doorbell rang, and a man identified himself as a policeman. Mutti opened the door a crack, and I spoke to him with the chain on. They had evidently arrested the man.

When Mrs. Malinow came home, we told her what had happened. She felt terrible that she had locked up the phone and apologized again. We told her that, under the circumstances, we would be moving as soon as possible.

Within a week we found another furnished room in Washington Heights on 168th Street. Our new landlady, Mrs. Fischbein, was in her seventies, with a deep, very masculine voice. Everyone who called us on her telephone thought we were living with a man. She happily gave us kitchen privileges and allowed us to use her telephone. She particularly enjoyed her Yiddish discussions with Mutti, for Mutti's English still wasn't too fluent. We stayed there for about a year.

Chapter 40

Mutti and I began job hunting almost as soon as we hit New York. On Ruth's advice, we started at the New York State Employment Office.

They told me that, since I was only sixteen years old and did not have a high school diploma, I would have to go to Continuation School once a week, where I could take a business course if I wanted to. They also had a position for me.

I explained that I was only three months short of receiving my diploma in Shanghai and would like to finish school at night so that I could get an American diploma. I was told that I would have to go to night school for two full years to make up those three months.

I enrolled at George Washington High School to fulfill this requirement, But when I was docked points for British spelling—*colour* instead of *color, licence* for *license*—I was so disgusted with the unfairness of it all, that I quit at the end of the term. I waited twenty-five years to receive an American high school diploma.

NYANA arranged for me to take night-time secretarial courses at a business school in the Times Square area. Mutti, in the meantime, had enrolled in night school to perfect her English and during the day worked in a camera factory.

I did not know it at the time, but Mark Cross Fifth Avenue was one of the most prestigious leather and luggage stores in New York. The secretarial position that I was being interviewed for was in their credit department at Broadway and 66th Street.

This was going to be my first job, and I was going to try not to sound too British. I had discovered that Americans were not too fond of foreign accents. Mrs. Conway was the credit manager, and I would be her secretary. She gave me a typing and shorthand test and was amazed at how well I did. I was hired on the spot at the enormous salary (to me) of $28 a week. I would have to work every other Saturday.

This presented a dilemma. I was still a Sabbath observer, and now I had to break the rules every other week. However, I needed the job, and so I had to go along with these rules. It was a pleasant job. I made friends immediately and was promoted quickly. I learned to operate the Monroe calculator and the comptometer, the manual teletype machine for credit information, and the switchboard. I got to know which customers paid their bills promptly and which ones had to be dunned. When I became Mrs. Conway's assistant, I even gave credit approval over the telephone. Within two years, I received several raises and was soon making $37 per week.

Mutti had gotten in touch with her nephew Ruben Beatus in Palestine. (I still remembered the spinach incident when they had stopped off in Breslau.) He also gave us the sad news that his parents (his mother Frieda was Mutti's sister) had perished in the gas chambers, as had his only sister with her son.

This sister was married and had a little boy. Only her husband had gotten a visa for the United States. She had to wait till he could send her an affidavit. When she received it, she booked passage for herself and her little son on a Dutch ship. They managed to get to Amsterdam. The very day of the ship's departure, Hitler invaded Holland. Her husband felt so guilt-ridden that he never remarried.

Ruben told us that his brother Jacob, now living in Wales, was visiting New York, and that his other brother Salo (Sam) had gotten divorced in Palestine and was now living in Jackson Heights, Queens, with his new wife Edith.

We were thrilled to have family again so close by, and immediately contacted them. We were most warmly welcomed by these cousins as well as by Edith's parents, with whom they were presently living. They had also just heard of a small apartment that had become vacant in a two-family house, on Forley Street, in the neighboring community of Elmhurst, and thought we might be interested in having our own apartment. We thought that was great. It was 1948, and there was still a housing shortage.

We went to look at it, and even though it was a basement apartment, it had a private entrance and the windows were above ground level. There was a large bedroom/living-room combination, eat-in kitchen, and a bathroom with shower.

Mrs. Urnstein, a widow, was the owner. She was a German gentile who was forced to flee Germany in the thirties with her Jewish husband. She and Mutti had an immediate rapport.

During the ghetto years in Shanghai, I became prone to severe cases of tonsillitis coupled with a high temperature. The doctor had wanted me to have another tonsillectomy; in Germany my tonsils had only been clipped, rather than scraped, and they had grown back. Yet, he advised me to delay this surgery until it could be done under better sanitary and climatic conditions.

When my bouts with tonsillitis continued after our arrival in the United States, I waited for an opportune moment to take care of the problem. I was now eighteen years old, with full insurance coverage through my job, and thus I entered the Polyclinic Hospital in Manhattan. It was not a very pleasant surgery, though this time, of course, I was well aware of what was going on.

Mutti was looking around for another job. The commute to the camera factory in the Bronx was too long. She answered an ad in the *Aufbau* (Reconstruction), a German Jewish newspaper, which had been founded by refugees arriving in New York in 1938–1939. It was universally read by the German Jewish community. People inserted want ads, marriages, birth announcements, and obituaries. It was one way of keeping in touch with what once was.

This particular ad stated that a Mr. Bauernfreund was looking for a forelady to work in his powder puff factory. Because the factory was in Corona, twenty minutes from our apartment in Elmhurst, Mutti quickly answered the ad. It seems she was everything—and more—that Mr. Bauernfreund was looking for. Mutti did not consider this a come-down for a former owner of a business, on the contrary, she was so happy to get this position that we went out to celebrate.

The job consisted of supervising a staff of about thirty Italian women who spoke very little English (and Mutti did not speak Italian), who were stuffing talcum powder into puffs and mitts and were getting paid for piece work. At fifty-seven, Mutti was starting a new way of life.

Chapter 41

It was time for me to move on. I had outgrown my job at Mark Cross, and I felt I could do better financially elsewhere.

Mutti and I had paid back our financial obligations to NYANA, and I had a pretty good social life. I was seeing many of my Shanghai friends who had settled in New York, and we had started an organization of former Shanghailanders at the YM-YWHA of Washington Heights.

My new job was as secretary at the Overseas Metal & Ore Corporation situated on Broadway, near the Battery. I was earning $65 a week. In the fall of 1950, I enrolled in the evening program of the City College of New York's School of Journalism as a non-matriculated student.

The Abbey Institute on 54th Street in New York, a small private school where my cousin Sam had studied advertising, was offering courses in copy writing and conversational French. I always wanted to perfect my high school French, and copy writing seemed to provide an opening for getting into the advertising field.

This was to be a turning point in my life, for Abbey Institute is where I met Harold Pike, and it was love at first sight.

Harold was also living in Queens—with his mother, stepfather, sister, and a stepbrother. American-born, World War II veteran, graduate of Brooklyn College, he was starting medical school in Geneva, Switzerland, in the fall.

Unfortunately, the American medical schools, as well as some other institutions of learning, still had a so-called quota system. It was still difficult for Jews, as well as some other minorities, to be admitted. After being turned down by various American schools, Harold applied to overseas schools that were accepting Americans.

He proposed six weeks after our first date, Memorial Day 1950. He wanted me to wait for him till he completed school and could support me properly, but I didn't want to wait for five years, and I told him I would not mind working. We got engaged on my twentieth birthday. He was going to Geneva as planned, would look for an apartment, and return the following May, at the end of the first semester, at which time we would get married. We would both work in New York during the summer, and the savings would help support us in Geneva till I got a job there.

Mutti was very unhappy with these arrangements. She did not like the idea of my going back to Europe for five years, even though it was Switzerland, particularly because she was going to be left alone. I felt bad about that too, but I thought I had found my American dream.

Harold's family was not too thrilled with our plans either. His stepfather was kind and noncommittal, but his mother, who had come to the United States from Russia in 1922, did not like me at all. I had three strikes against me: I was a refugee, I was from Germany, and I was penniless. She thought I was after her son's money, for he would be a doctor within five years. The fact that I would actually be working to put him through medical school didn't enter into the discussion.

How had Harold figured on supporting himself and paying the tuition on his own? His idea had been to use up the rest of his GI Bill eligibility, which would get him through the first year in Switzerland, and subsequently he would come home to work every other year to earn his tuition and living expenses.

We both insisted that ours was the right decision, and against both of our parents' objections, decided to go ahead with our plans. Harold had booked passage in the *Ile de France* leaving for Le Havre on August 19.

However, again a war was going to disrupt my life.

Chapter 42

On June 25, 1950, North Korean Communist troops invaded South Korea. On June 27, President Truman ordered U.S. air and naval forces to help defend South Korea, and on June 30, American ground troops were sent in. There was now talk in the news about the possibility of World War III.

How was this going to affect our wedding plans, we wondered. If there was another war, I would be in Europe, as a stateless person again, and I definitely could not take that risk.

Quickly, we decided that we would have to get married before his departure. To become a United States citizen usually requires a five-year residency. For the spouse of a citizen it is only three years. I was now a three-year resident.

Mutti, resigned to my decision, quickly called Rabbi Breuer, the German Jewish Orthodox rabbi, and arranged for him to marry us in his Washington Heights study, sometime in August. My future mother-in-law was aghast. Her son to be married in a rabbi's study, with just the family present? No hall, no party, no band, no relatives invited? No way.

Mutti explained to her that she didn't have the funds to make a big wedding. She was barely able to make ends meet as it was, and had just repaid her loans from the Joint. Making a big wedding was an absolute impossibility. Take a loan, she was told. A wedding loan? She had never heard of such a thing. Except for the relocation loan from the Joint, she had never been in debt, and she was not going to get into debt now. She was very firm about that.

Harold and I were caught in the middle. I would have liked a nice wedding, but I knew we could not afford it. Harold realized that too, but he did not want to offend his mother either.

We hit upon a compromise. How about getting married by a judge, not tell anyone, except our parents, and postpone the "big" wedding for a year? Our plans for Harold's return the following May would still stand, and in the meantime I could apply for citizenship papers. It would take months to process my naturalization papers anyway. I could continue working and expected a generous

Christmas bonus from my firm. By pooling our funds, we could then be married in a synagogue, have a little reception, and I could go to Geneva with him in the fall protected by my new American passport.

Harold's mother agreed, provided no one else was in on the plan, (so we would not be deprived of any gifts when we had our "real" wedding the following year). Mutti was still unhappy even with these plans, but she agreed that I had to make my own life.

On August 18, 1950, we went to City Hall for a marriage license, got our blood tests and then were married in Judge Benjamin Shalleck's living room, on Riverside Drive, during my lunch hour. His wife and maid were the two required witnesses.

Harold left for Europe the following day, and the day after I filed for my American citizenship papers.

Harold had adjusted well to Geneva and his schooling. I received wonderful, long letters, at least twice a week describing the city to me and telling me how much he missed me. He was hoping to come home to New York at the end of the semester in May, and then we would have our Jewish wedding, as planned.

As it turned out, this was not to be. In January of 1951, Mutti received a phone call from Harold's mother, who wanted to know how far the "wedding plans" had progressed. Mutti told her again that she would be able to arrange the wedding at the Hebrew Tabernacle located in upper Manhattan, and a small reception for family, and possibly a few friends afterwards. I was already looking for an inexpensive wedding dress. All this would take her savings as well as mine, only leaving enough money to purchase my steamship ticket to Europe.

But, my mother-in-law was adamant. Unless Mutti took out a loan of at least $2,000 to make a "proper" wedding, she would not pay for Harold's return ticket, and therefore there would be no wedding here.

I wrote to Harold explaining all these difficulties and suggested that I would pay for his roundtrip ticket out of the savings, and we could still be married by a rabbi in New York, forgoing any reception. I wanted Mutti to be at my wedding. However, he agreed with his mother that without a "big" reception it would not be worthwhile for him to return in May.

On February 20, I pledged allegiance to the flag of the United States of America in the federal court in Brooklyn. I was now a full-fledged American citizen, with an American passport—a very precious document.

I now had to make one of the most difficult decisions of my life. I wanted Mutti to walk down the aisle at my wedding so badly, but that wasn't possible if I was going to marry Harold whom I was madly in love with.

With a heavy heart, I said good-bye to a tearful Mutti, and on March 7 set sail on the *Ile de France* for Le Havre, to a new life and marriage to a young man whom I had only dated for four months and had not seen in seven.

I was going back to Europe, the continent I had left as a refugee twelve years previously.

PART VI

Hiatus
1951–1975

Chapter 43

Geneva, Switzerland, March 1951

It was an exciting trip. I practiced my high school French and met some American medical students who were also going to Geneva and would be in Harold's classes. He and I had our reunion at the Gare St. Lazare in Paris.

This was my first trip to Paris and I tried to imagine my Uncle Leo living there. I went to the Sûreté the next day to get more information on his deportation. They were able to find his files, as well as the Nazi documentation of the confiscation of his place of business, his carte d'identitée, and confirmation of the date of his arrest, July 19, 1942.

(In 1978, French Nazi hunters Beate and Serge Klarsfeld compiled a book, *Le Memorial de la déportation des juifs de France*, documenting the names of 67,000 Jews who were deported from France. Uncle Leo and my cousin Ruben Nelken had been sent to the holding camp at Drancy. They were deported to Auschwitz on Convoy 25 on August 28, 1942. There were 957 persons in this convoy. Only 17 survived. My uncle and cousin were not among them.)

A letter from Mutti awaited me in Geneva, in which she informed me that she had just heard from Israel that we had Swiss cousins, fortuitously residing in Geneva. Bébé Goldfarb's grandfather had been my grandfather Avrohom's brother, and Mutti remembered Bébé's father very well.

Bébé, and her brother Richard were Parisian born. Richard had been hidden during the war by the maquis, the French underground, and had for a time even been with Uncle Leo. Bébé had married Joseph Goldfarb, a genevois, and was living in Geneva. Her parents had been issued forged passports by the maquis in Lyons, and thereby escaped deportation.

On March 27, 1951, I walked down the aisle of the Geneva synagogue, sorely missing Muti.

Because my dream had always been to retrace my parents' steps on my honeymoon, off to Vienna we went.

Chapter 44

The Vienna we saw was not at all what Mutti had described. Not only was much of it in ruins, but the people were poorly dressed, and the ravages of war could be seen everywhere. The city was occupied by the four powers, United States, France, Britain, and the Soviet Union, but we had permission to go into all sectors. I looked up some former Shanghai friends who had returned to Vienna, and they showed us around the city.

It was exciting to be honeymooning in the same city that my parents had honeymooned in twenty-two years before. At the time, the part the Austrians played in accepting the Nazis so readily had not been well publicized, and we did not realize that these people were as bad as the Germans in persecuting and helping deport their Jews. (This was many years before Kurt Waldheim became Secretary General of the U.N. Had we known, we would never had visited that country.)

On our return to Geneva, an invitation from the Goldfarbs to join them at the forthcoming Passover seders was waiting for us. I was thrilled to meet some more of my family. The only cousins I had met as an adult were Jacob and Sam.

This was my first experience at a seder conducted almost totally in French. Only the blessings were recited in Hebrew, and then we all read from a French *Haggadah.* Because my French was not proficient enough, I read my part in Hebrew.

Harold had rented a beautiful apartment in a new building on the rue de Carouge. All the furniture, including the stove, had been purchased at the *marché de puce* (flea market). As foreigners, we were not permitted a lease in a rent-controlled building so this apartment did not come cheap. I had to start job hunting quickly. Harold's G.I. bill money was going to run out the following year.

I first applied for a secretarial position at the American Consulate. Strangely enough they only employed local Swiss nationals in that position. Even though I was qualified, it was a detriment that I was an American.

In order for me to get a Swiss working permit, I had to find an employer who could prove to the authorities that he could not get a Swiss to perform the same type of work.

Switzerland is a quatrolingual country: French, German, Italian, and Romansh (a form of Latin) being spoken in four different sections of the country. Geneva is situated in the French section. I decided to seek a bilingual secretarial position for I knew that Swiss-Germans were moving to Geneva to improve their French and chose to seek positions requiring French only. It was therefore difficult for firms to find German speaking secretaries willing to work in that language.

Within a short period of time I found a very interesting, though low-paid job with a syndicated columnist, whose customers were Swiss-German newspapers. My job was to type his German articles and take care of his English correspondence.

Mr. and Mrs. Wyler were Swiss-German Jews and ran the business out of their home in Champel, on the city outskirts at the top of a big hill. They both also spoke English and French. It was a pretty long trip by tram and bus, so I purchased a *vélomoteur*, a moped, which would easily make the uphill trip. I felt lucky having this position, for most of the other job-hunting wives were unsuccessful.

One day, arriving at the Wylers', I experienced a sharp pain in my side. Mrs. Wyler thought that I might have a burst ovarian cyst and quickly drove me to a female surgeon she knew. By the time we got there, the pain was so intense I could hardly move.

The surgeon's diagnosis was a burst appendix, which required immediate surgery. Harold was permitted to be present at the operation, but there wasn't time to telegraph Mutti and before I knew it, I was in Geneva's Catholic Hospital, and woke up to find Jesus on a big wooden cross, staring at me from above my bed.

The sisters were very efficient, but brusque. It seemed that it had been pretty much touch-and-go with me. When the surgeon started operating, she found the appendix intact, yet I was hemorrhaging badly from somewhere. An ectopic pregnancy was considered, yet that's not what it was either. I had a burst ovarian cyst, and *Madame la doctoresse* was able to repair it. Ironically, Mrs. Wyler's layman's diagnosis had probably saved my life.

Every week Mutti sent us the Sunday papers with the comics,

which were then passed around the American student colony, now some two hundred strong. Into it she would sneak either a hard salami, nylons, or some little trinket—the paper never arrived empty. Now, while I was recuperating from my surgery, she managed to add some other goodies. I felt bad that she couldn't be with me, even though the Goldfarbs and the other students were most helpful and came to visit me often.

The school term was over in May, so we booked passage on the SS *Queen Elizabeth* for New York.

Chapter 45

May 1952. It felt great to be back in the good old U.S.A. again, and of course to see Mutti. She had been so worried about my operation, and now at least she could see that I was fully recuperated and none the worse for wear. She was still working in the powderpuff factory, but had taken up smoking, about a pack a day. I could see that she was very lonely with me so far away, even though, right after our departure, Aunt Henny, now in New York, had moved in with her.

During our four months at home, we stayed with my in-laws. Harold got a summer job at the Post Office, and I got a pretty well paying secretarial position with the Mosler Safe Company, commuting to Manhattan by bus and subway.

We saved every cent—the G.I. Bill monies had finally run out. In the fall we returned to Europe on the maiden voyage of the SS *United States* and, through a mix up, they gave us a stateroom. We reveled traveling in style on a luxury ship, making its maiden voyage.

After debarking in Southampton, we went on to London, staying at the Regency Palace Hotel in Picadilly Circus. Again, I saw a war's devastation in Europe, for much of London was still in ruins and the city was very somber. Then we returned to Geneva, and, my position at the Wylers' having been filled, I was hired by the World Alliance of YMCAs. Mr. Guiness, an Englishman, was the editor of the monthly magazine. He spoke only English and was delighted to have a trilingual secretary. We had many interesting discussions on religion—he said he was particularly fascinated with Judaism—his parents had both been missionaries. I was an oddity—the only Jewish person on the staff.

In 1954, the Intergovernmental Committee for European Migration (ICEM) was being established in Geneva. I had heard that secretarial positions were paying extremely well, up to $2,300 per annum, so I sent in an application for employment. After receiving my security clearance, I was hired for the position of comptometer operator in the Finance Department. Because of my knowledge of German, however, I was soon recommended for the position of trilingual secretary to the director of the whole division, who was a German. This was the first time as an adult that I came face to face with a German.

During the interview, I sat in a chair opposite his desk, and he spoke to me in English. He asked where I was born and where I had been during the war. Speaking English put me a little at ease, and yet I could not help wondering where *he* was during the war. Did he gas any Jews? Could he have shot any little children? What did he do? Of course, from my reply, he immediately realized that I was Jewish. He was most polite when he asked me to work for him as his personal secretary.

Even though I had mixed feelings, I decided to give it a try.

It was then that I had my first unpleasant encounter. It was with his very Aryan assistant, a woman in her early thirties. Whereas my boss took pains to converse with me in English only (most of the work I did for him was in English), this person, though fluent in English, always chose to speak to me in German. Inevitably, one day, the war came up in discussion. She mentioned that she had been in the *Hitlerjugend*, and then remarked that it was all propaganda about six million Jews being murdered by the Nazis.

"Impossible," she declared. "Maybe a few thousand died in the camps, but many more good Germans lost their lives during the American bombardments."

I was flabbergasted. Obviously Nazism, and anti-Semitism had not died with the fall of Germany. I told her flatly that, in my family alone, eighty relatives had perished. She looked astounded and never brought up the subject again.

Chapter 46

Harold and I had purchased a 1951 Prefect (the British equivalent of a Ford), with a floor clutch and in order to downshift from third to second gear, it was necessary to double-clutch.

As soon as I received my driver's license, we took some small trips, to France, Spain, Italy, staying in cheap hotels. Our vacation fund consisted of all the money gifts which we received for birthdays and anniversaries from home.

Whereas it had taken me about a half hour on my *vélomoteur* to get to work, it was only ten minutes by car. Harold went to school, which was just a few minutes away, on his bicycle. He did all the grocery shopping and most of the cooking. The stores closed at 6:00 P.M. and I worked till that time. He usually got home around four o'clock. We had a nice social life with the American students, most of whom received monetary support from their families. We were one of the few who didn't. We also had some Swiss friends.

Our first child, Marilyn May, was born on July 9, 1955, at the Clinique Bois Gentil. ICEM had a very good health plan, and I was able to take off twelve weeks after the birth, with full pay, after which we hired a Swiss nurse to take care of the baby during my working hours.

Mutti's telegram reflected her excitement on becoming a grandmother for the first time. As soon as I became pregnant, she had sent us a complete baby layette. Again, I missed having her with me to share in this moment.

Because my mother-in-law was almost illiterate, Harold's step-father took care of all the correspondence to us. His letters reflected their happiness on becoming grandparents for the first time, and were looking forward to our return home.

Never having been around infants, I had to learn to take care of one from the ground up. There was no ready-made baby food available, nor was there any diaper service, and of course this was long before the day of disposable diapers. I had a hand pureer, and Mutti had sent a large supply of cloth diapers. I bought a huge pot and a long-handled wooden spoon, and every night I boiled diapers.

On December 24, 1955, right after medical school graduation, we boarded the SS *America* in Southampton for the five-day voyage home.

Chapter 47

New York, December 29, 1955

The sight of Mutti waiting at the pier for a glimpse of her first grandchild, on a bitterly cold winter day, will forever be etched in my memory. She was first in line as we came down the gangplank with little Marilyn in a carry-crib, all bundled up with only her eyes peering out from the top. Mutti had just turned sixty-four and didn't look a day over fifty. She carried the baby into the warm waiting room, where my in-laws were waiting for us, while we sorted out our luggage.

Aunt Henny had moved into an apartment within a few blocks of Mutti's, which made it convenient for us to move into her apartment temporarily. Harold had been accepted at Flushing Hospital for his internship starting July 1. Not wanting to waste any time, he accepted a six-month internship at New Rochelle Hospital, starting January 1. In those days internships paid very little—$150 per month.

In April we moved into a three-room garden apartment in Kew Gardens Hills. I was doing home typing for some people, but it wasn't enough to cover our expenses. The rent alone was $85 a month. Mutti worked full-time but would baby-sit for us occasionally when we wanted to go out for the evening. My in-laws owned a laundry and dry-cleaning business on the Lower East Side of Manhattan where my mother-in-law worked three days. She offered to care for Marilyn the other two days if I could find a part-time job. Fortunately, my secretarial skills came in handy again. I got a job as a legal secretary in Manhattan.

One day, I received a call from Flushing Hospital that Mutti had been taken there after a fall in the subway. She had just gotten up to leave the train when it gave a sudden jerk, and she had banged her head. She could not remember her name or where she lived, but she had identification with her, so they were able to reach us. Luckily the amnesia was only temporary.

After a stay of a few days and some tests, the doctors allowed her to go home. They attributed the amnesia to the extreme heat we had been exposed to in Shanghai.

Mutti had applied for restitution payments from Germany. Konrad Adenauer, the first Chancellor of postwar Germany, had instituted the reparations agreement, whereby victims of Nazi persecution could claim financial return for stolen property, bank accounts, etc.

Her restitution lawyer was also making application to probate Uncle Leo's will, which named her sole beneficiary. She had the necessary proof of his deportation to Auschwitz. The Nazis had confiscated all his property, which consisted of an apartment, furniture, and his business. Mutti inherited the aggregate amount approved under the German *Wiedergutmachung* ruling.

She then broke a promise she had made to herself never to set foot on German soil again. On her way to Switzerland, she stopped off in Munich, on her lawyer's advice, for the probation of Uncle Leo's will. Right after her court appearance, she took the first plane out of Germany, for her emotional state would not allow her to spend even a night in that country. She told me that when she drank a cup of coffee at the Munich airport, she almost choked on it.

As the widow of a World War I veteran, Mutti received a monthly widow's pension. Because the business had been solely in her name, she was eligible to receive one hundred percent in German social security benefits. How happy she was that she had had the foresight to subscribe back in 1933.

Over the years, her other claims were also approved. Of course she only received a fraction of the value of the confiscated property. Both of us received small sums for the eight years spent in Shanghai.

This income gave her the opportunity to retire after celebrating her sixty-seventh birthday. She was now going to travel and spend some time with her grandchildren.

And travel she did. With her numerous widowed friends she went to Israel, Russia, Poland, Hungary, Czechoslovakia, Denmark, Holland, Sweden, Italy, France, England, and across America. She had joined the German Jewish Congregation Habonim in Manhattan, where she taught canasta, and then at age seventy-five took up the game of bridge. She would have three or four weekly games going.

Her greatest enjoyment was in spending the Jewish holidays with us and attending services in our synagogue. During our Passover seders, she would tell us stories about the seders in her parents' home which, according to her, never ended. She remembered her Hebrew well as she read passages from the *Haggadah.*

Often she would say, "if only Vati could have lived. He would have enjoyed every moment—he loved you so much, Evelinchen."

I felt lucky that Mutti's perseverance and ingenuity had helped us survive the Holocaust. In turn I was dedicating myself to Jewish causes. Mutti and I were in Madison Square Garden the night Israel became a State. At my synagogue, I helped organize demonstrations to free Soviet Jews. I needed to do what had not been done for us in the 1930s.

Chapter 48

On August 31, 1958 we bought our dream house in Jericho, Long Island—a beautiful four–bedroom split with a formal dining room and a cathedral-ceiling living room. The best part was the master bedroom which had a dressing room attached and a huge walk-in closet. Mutti lent us the down payment out of her German reparations funds.

Our son, Sheldon Bruce, was born on October 31, and on February 27, 1959, we moved into our new home and joined the local Conservative synagogue where I became an active member.

After Harold completed his internship at Flushing Hospital he had to make a decision on a residency program. Everything still paid very little. He was considering obstetrics or general surgery. However, when a psychiatric residency became available at Creedmoor State Hospital, he decided to try it. He could always get some credit for the training should he decide at a future time to go into a different specialty. One consideration was that this residency paid much more than any of the others and was only for three years. He subsequently became Supervising Psychiatrist.

We had purposely picked a corner house so that Harold could establish a psychiatric practice working out of our home. As it turned out, by choice it would always be a part-time practice. I managed the office—making patient appointments, doing the billing, bookkeeping, correspondence and filling out insurance forms. My hours were my own and therefore very flexible. This allowed me to be available for the children, for I remembered how Mutti always tried to be home for me during our difficult years in Shanghai.

About a year later, Harold was appointed Assistant Director at what was later to become the Suffolk Developmental Center. He had evening office hours three times a week and when we started to live very comfortably having hired sleep-in help, I became pregnant with my third child.

Doreen Belinda was born in 1961 followed by Sheryl Pauline in 1962. We had always wanted four children, so our family was now complete.

Mutti accompanied us on all our winter vacations and baby-sat whenever we took trips on our own. Even though we had the sleep-in help it was still a tremendous responsibility to supervise four little children, particularity at her advanced age. But nothing fazed her. The children absolutely adored her. She would regale them with stories of her childhood, growing up in pre-radio and pre-television Germany.

She would play "*Hoppa, hoppa Reiter,*" while bouncing them on her knee, or tell them the story of *Rotköpfchen* (Little Red Riding Hood) in German, as well as many others from her childhood and mine. A favorite was from Humperdinck's opera Hansel and Gretel— "*Ein Männlein steht im Walde ganz still und stumm. . . .*" I taught them the Hebrew *Shema* prayer, and when she visited, she would recite it with them before putting them to sleep.

In 1964, the temple's Sisterhood honored me with a surprise "This Is Your Life" program. The kids were there and excited to stay up so late. Harold wrote a beautiful poem and the organizers managed to bring in many former Shanghailanders as part of the festivities. But I think Mutti was the star—she contributed so much to the story, she might as well have written it herself. She took such pride in her family.

Not having been raised at a time when girls had a Bat Mitzvah, Mutti was thrilled when Marilyn had her Bat Mitzvah in 1968. She shared in the joy of Sheldon's Bar Mitzvah in 1971, and then Doreen's Bat Mitzvah in 1974.

In February 1975 our winter vacation was spent in St. Thomas in a beautiful house on a hill overlooking the pool.

Little did we know the shock that awaited all of us just a few months later.

PART VII

Aftermath

1985 reunion of former Shanghailanders at Concord Hotel, Kiamesha Lake, New York, attended by hundreds. Author in center holding banner.

Chapter 49

Memorial Day 1975

"I am leaving," Harold announced out of the blue.

"Leaving?" I asked, "Where are you going?"

It was 3 o'clock in the afternoon of the holiday weekend and we had promised the children we would take them shopping.

Before he could answer, the office doorbell rang. Who could that be, I wondered? This was a holiday weekend. Harold raced down the stairs. I heard him open the door, but he did not return.

After a while, I looked out and saw him in a car with a woman. To say that I was in shock is putting it mildly.

It was the end of my marriage.

Over the last few years I had noticed a change in my husband. It happened gradually after he failed a director's exam given at the New York State Department of Mental Hygiene. He became despondent, moody and short-tempered, even with the children. He decided he really did not like psychiatry. He would prefer being a family doctor. I told him that was fine with me. I would get a full-time job while he took additional hospital training. He was afraid it would curtail our lifestyle which, though comfortable, was not exorbitant.

He took a leave of absence from his hospital job to work in a bariatric practice (weight control), then opened his own office. I was his office manager and assistant. If he did well, he was going to give up his hospital job.

I did not know he was floundering, and it never dawned on me that he was having an affair with one of his psychiatric patients.

Harold stated that he did not want a divorce, but wanted to live with his mistress and stay married.

This was unacceptable to me. However, shortly after filing for divorce, I agreed to a reconciliation. The spark and the trust had gone, but I still loved my husband and hoped this 24-year-old marriage could be saved. Mutti was in Europe for the summer and luckily did not know what was going on. My mother-in-law, now widowed, supported me wholeheartedly and was angry with her son.

"You are just like a daughter to me," she said.

Marilyn had gotten engaged on my birthday and was getting married November 2. Right after the invitations went out, her future father-in-law was hospitalized. He had a long recuperation ahead and would be too weak to participate in the wedding and reception. Marilyn and her fiancé did not want to postpone the ceremony, so it was decided that they would get married in the rabbi's study with only the immediate family present, and would have the big wedding and reception at our synagogue the following February.

It seemed like history was repeating itself, for it was not to be.

Sheryl's Bat Mitzvah took place December 19. It was a wonderful evening. Everyone looked great. Mutti glowed. I had never mentioned my problems to her. Why worry her if everything is okay.

Chapter 50

It was New Year's Eve, and we had a dinner appointment with some close friends. While I waited for Harold to come home from the hospital, I dressed, beginning to get worried by his delay. We're going to be late, I was thinking when the phone rang.

"I am here for a drink," said Harold.

"Where is 'here'?" I asked him.

"I'll be back when I am ready to come back," was his only reply.

Our friends waited with me, but when Harold had not appeared by eleven o'clock, they took me home with them. He returned the next afternoon and was surprised that I would not let him in. As far as I was concerned, this was *it*—the end.

My only problem was how to tell Mutti. This will kill her, I thought.

I asked a close friend who spoke German to come with me to tell Mutti. It was not easy. She felt sorry for me, but she was quite angry that I had never said anything to her during our seven months of reconciliation. I told her I had not wanted to worry her, in case the reconciliation worked. However, what got her particularly upset was that the day before, December 30, Harold had borrowed a sum of money from her to be used as down payment on a bariatric practice in Manhattan. This was to be repaid out of the proceeds of the new practice.

Under the circumstances, Mutti was afraid that she would never see her money again and requested that it be returned to her immediately. However, Harold refused.

His reasoning for the refusal may have been based on an insurance settlement following a 1972 accident I had been in, taking Mutti home after Passover. Someone ran a light and totaled my car, and Mutti, in the front passenger seat, though wearing a seat belt, ended up with multiple injuries, and spent weeks in intensive care at a local hospital. She had just turned eighty, and things didn't look too good for her. But she had the strength and will power to get back on her feet again.

Harold was involved in settling the lawsuit that followed the accident. My share of the compensation was very small, because I had only been slightly injured. Mutti received the larger share, and Harold felt that she should give us some of the proceeds because we had to buy a new car. He was angry when I would not ask her for the money. Possibly he now thought the money he had borrowed from her was due him.

It almost killed her having to take him to court. She had trusted him, and her trust had been violated. The money was finally returned to her after a court trial, during which she gained the respect and admiration not only of both lawyers, but also of the judge.

Meanwhile Harold and I were divorced. At the hearing, the fact that I had managed my husband's office and had worked to send him through medical school, internship, and residency was taken into consideration. I was awarded adequate alimony and child support, which I received for a while. But suddenly the payments stopped, and Harold was cited for contempt of court.

During our marriage, Harold had always been a good husband and loving father. He was also a most ethical and conscientious doctor— and undoubtedly still is. It was totally incomprehensible to me why he would take such action—and subsequent actions, and completely out of character for the man I had once loved and been married to.

Divorce became my personal holocaust, another turning point in my tumultuous life. Just as Mutti had fought for our survival in Shanghai, I too was going to have to fight tooth and nail for my children's survival. I still had three children in high school, and Sheldon had been accepted at SUNY Albany. Though Marilyn never had the big wedding, I had seen to it that her college tuition was paid. In June 1976 she graduated from SUNY Stony Brook.

I took a job at Helena Rubinstein's as a trilingual secretary, but when the firm moved its offices to Manhattan two years later, it became unacceptable to commute. I needed to work locally in order to be available for my two younger children. I went on unemployment and hunted for another job. It was not easy to get a suitable position. All of a sudden I was "overqualified," which meant, in plain English, that they preferred hiring a younger person, because the firms would not have to pay them for qualifications and expertise.

I vividly remember one particularly humiliating experience. I was interviewed for a position as executive secretary requiring knowledge of French and German. I passed the interview and accompanying test with flying colors—but I did not get the job. Months afterward they were still advertising the job, listed with every employment agency where I registered. After much prodding, I finally ascertained from one of the agencies that the problem was my age, even though by law they were not allowed to say so.

To make ends meet, I had to do it all on my own. Mutti gave me some money now and then, but that couldn't go on for long—she had to hold on to her savings in case she became infirm. After all, she was now eighty-six years old. Also, I did not want to burden her with all my troubles. My divorce had already taken its toll on her. When Harold took my car out of the parking lot while I was at work (it was still registered in his name), she gave me some money to buy another car, because that was the only way I could get to work. When the mandated support money was not forthcoming, I applied for welfare, but they turned me down because the mortgage payments were $100 above their allotment; however, I was eligible for food stamps.

I never thought, when I left Shanghai, that I would ever want for food again. Yet here I was trying to make ends meet with the $94 per month in food stamps the government apportioned me to feed three people. Sheldon was on financial aid and received his own food stamps in college. I had to become as innovative as Mutti had been in Shanghai. One thing I would not do was sell my beautiful house. I was determined to keep that.

I had finally established roots in the community. I was not about to become a refugee again. Once was enough. Nor was I going to move my children away from their friends, school, and everything they knew. My roots had become their roots. The trauma of an absentee father and lack of amenities was enough of a burden on them.

I found that even institutions have a heart. When Harold got behind in the mortgage payments, which the court had mandated him to pay, and the bank wanted to foreclose, they let me defer some of the payments. When Long Island Lighting wanted to shut off my gas and electricity for the same reason, they also made some concessions for me. I even had my picture in *Newsday* with an accompanying story of my predicament.

One day I received a notice from Long Island Lighting and various enterprises addressed to Mrs. Pike, new homeowner, with a different first name than mine. Harold's half of the house had been signed over to the new Mrs. Pike. (He had married her in a civil ceremony after refusing to grant me a *get*, Jewish divorce. This document has to be obtained through a Bet Din, a Jewish court, and will only be granted with the consent of the husband.)

My former mother-in-law had a change of heart and cut off all communication between me and her grandchildren, previously kept open. She did not want to antagonize her son.

I literally worked seven days a week. I started a secretarial service, sold makeup, studied hypnosis, took in boarders, ran pool parties for singles—how fortunate for me that we had installed an in-ground pool in 1972—and was able to get some temporary office positions.

Doreen and Sheryl were now in two New York State colleges, receiving student loans and financial aid, and Sheldon was starting medical school at the Faculté de Médecine in Lille, France, after he was unable to get accepted at an American medical school. Being in a foreign school, he did not qualify for financial aid, only government student loans. The support money I sent him came from what I earned in my various enterprises. Mutti paid his rent.

Luckily, I still had one credit card, which had been issued in my name alone. All the others had been canceled. I used this card sparingly for the interest was high, but the monthly payments could be kept low. This Visa card enabled me to buy most of Sheldon's medical books.

Under New York State divorce law, I was permitted exclusive residency in the house in Jericho until my youngest child reached the age of eighteen. At that time I had to sell the house and split the proceeds or buy that half myself. After approximately six years of litigation I agreed to a settlement, whereby I received a fraction of the support arrears and that other half of the house, even though it was no longer in my ex-husband's name. With the court's permission, I then dropped all charges that had been leveled against him. But there was one item that I could not negotiate—the *get* was again refused.

In the meantime, Mutti was taking her summer vacations in Switzerland and Italy, mostly with her bridge-playing friends, and wintered in West Palm Beach. After her eighty-seventh birthday, she found the travel to Europe too tedious. Arthritis had set in, and she had trouble walking. She began spending her summers at Tennanah Lake Shore Lodge in Roscoe, New York.

I had become established as the director of the market research department of a commercial real estate company. One morning I received a call from Roscoe. Mutti had fallen, I was informed, and was disoriented. Doreen and Sheryl immediately drove up there, brought her back to Long Island, and had her admitted to a local hospital.

It turned out, she had slipped, fallen, and broken an elbow. There wasn't much they could do for her in the hospital, but it was obvious she could no longer live alone. The hospital rushed her out into a nursing home, before we were able to make any other arrangements for her.

It was supposed to be the finest nursing home in the area—it should have been, at $95 a day, not covered by Medicare. But after my first visit there, I thought I would collapse. Because she needed physical care as a wheelchair patient, she was placed in the unit that contained all the senile patients. Her mind, which was as sharp as ever, could not handle that. Neither could mine.

She insisted on going back to her apartment. After some trial and error, we hired Lucy, who immediately took charge. Lucy went with her to the lodge the following summer, and accompanied her wherever she wanted to go in a hired car. She was still playing bridge as avidly as ever.

Memorial Day 1983 she suffered a stroke and lapsed into a coma. The doctor warned us that she would not last through the night. Miraculously, the next morning she came out of the coma, but had lost her speech and was paralyzed on one side. The following week, she regained her speech, and the paralysis disappeared.

In November I got engaged to Leonard Rubin, an accountant and a recent widower, whom I met at a bridge game. A veteran of the Korean War, he had been stationed in Germany while I was living in Geneva. His mother and I established an immediate close relationship. His daughter Debra was a recent law school graduate, and his other daughter, Amy, was engaged to be married the following May.

He and Mutti hit it off immediately the moment they met. "Leonard," she said, pronouncing the name the German way, *"ist ein feiner Mann."*

On June 6, 1984, my indomitable Mutti became a great-grandmother. Marilyn had given birth to beautiful little Jocelyn, whom Mutti promptly dubbed "Pupperle (little doll)."

Two weeks later I married Lenny. I had been unsuccessful in obtaining a *get*, and not for lack of trying. Even Rabbi Avi Weiss, whom I had gone to see personally, was unable to help me. Unhappily, I had to reconcile myself to a traditional ceremony, conducted by a Reform rabbi. As it turned out, I could not have asked for a more beautiful, or meaningful ceremony, for the rabbi was a close friend, married to my childhood friend from Shanghai, Susie Kushner.

When Sheryl wheeled Mutti toward the *chuppah* in my backyard, her cup truly had run over. "Finally," she said, "I can be present at my own child's wedding. To see Evelyn happy is all I've ever wanted to live for. I am now at peace. This is the culmination of my own American Dream. *Du hast meinen schönsten Traum erfüllt."*

Mutti died on May 13, 1985, six months short of her ninety-fourth birthday, with Sheldon and myself at her side. He had just completed his medical school training.

The doctor had already called for the ambulance, for it seemed that she had never fully recovered from the pneumonia she had contracted six months earlier, at which time she had to undergo a tracheotomy. She stopped breathing before the ambulance had a chance to arrive. Sheldon tried CPR and mouth-to-mouth resuscitation. Her unconquerable heart had finally given out.

The day before, the whole family had been with her to celebrate Mother's Day. She mentioned that she didn't think she'd have the strength to attend the upcoming celebrations of Sheldon's medical school graduation, his wedding in June, Doreen's wedding in September, and Sheryl's engagement to Paul.

"Just hang in there, Grandma," they told her as she was holding Pupperle on her lap this one last time.

Just before we left, she called me into her room. "I am tired," she whispered, "but I want to tell you how happy you've all made me today. And you, Evelyn, have been a wonderful daughter to me. What you've done has been more than I ever thought you'd be able to, and you've had such a difficult time. You and I are survivors. When you get your book published, our story must also include your own struggles and the happy ending. Maybe I've never told you how much I appreciate having a daughter like you. But I want to tell you now!"

• • •

She had experienced success, when she started her own business, joy, when she married Vati, and more joy when she gave birth to her only child. She had experienced frustration when the Nazis stole everything she had worked for, satisfaction that she had been able to save her child, husband, and mother-in-law by arranging the flight to Shanghai. She experienced tragedy when she became widowed after only twelve short years of marriage. She demonstrated monumental fortitude and ingenuity in keeping the two of us alive during our years of deprivation. She had the stamina to start anew in America, and in her golden years she was finally able to live in peace and comfort.

Author with her four children. Left to right: Sheryl, Sheldon, Author, Doreen, Marilyn

STATE OF NEW YORK
EXECUTIVE CHAMBER
ALBANY 12224

MARIO M. CUOMO
GOVERNOR

January 20, 1993

To The Friends Of The 1993 UJA-Federation Annual Campaign:

On behalf of the Family of New York, I extend my best wishes to the UJA-Federation as you gather at the Jericho Jewish Center to launch this year's annual campaign.

Please allow me to join you in honoring Evelyn and Leonard Rubin, two outstanding New Yorkers. Together they have made a lasting, positive contribution to communal life on Long Island.

Evelyn Rubin deserves special praise for her tireless efforts to inform the public about her experiences during the Holocaust. Her personal testimony is inspiring. Public education helps insure that the world shall never again endure terror and tragedy of such epic proportions.

I commend you all for your efforts in support of the UJA-Federation, and I wish you success in this year's campaign.

Sincerely,

Mario M. Cuomo

ADDENDUM

When I decided to publish a second edition of GHETTO SHANGHAI, I thought it might be a good idea to clarify a few items that only came to light after the publication of the original edition. Some are minor, typographical errors, of interest to my family and some friends, and some just need clarification.

Actually, my father was born on June 6 and not June 7, (page 97), and the correct translation of Little Red Riding Hood should have been *Rotkäppchen* and not *Rotköpfchen,* which translates into Little Redhead (page 187). Also, when I indicated that the summer temperature in Shanghai might, at times, have reached an unbearable 140 degrees in the shade, it was in the context of present day measurement of the temperature/humidity index, (page 75).

With reference to the "Proclamation" that forced us to move into the Hongkew ghetto in 1943 (page 113), it has recently come to my attention that the arrival, in July 1942, of SS Col. Joseph Meisinger, the infamous "butcher of Warsaw," may have prompted this action on the part of the Japanese authorities. As the Gestapo representative in Tokyo, his mission was to rid Shanghai of the Jewish refugees who had escaped the Nazi clutches in Europe. His plan was to round up the Jews, possibly in synagogues on Rosh Hashanah and put us on ships out to sea where we would starve, or to incarcerate us in concentration camps, á la Europe.

Meisinger's murderous intentions, obviously, were never acted upon, due to the intervention of Japanese Vice Consul Shibota who was reluctant to follow through with this plan. Instead, he did acquiesce to a subsequent demand of his government's German allies to establish the Hongkew ghetto.

I wish to take this opportunity to thank the many readers who have contacted me by e-mail, as well as telephone and snail-mail from around the world. Some are former Shanghailanders who informed me how my story brought back memories – some fond, and some not so fond. Everyone remembered Ghoya, "King

i

of the Jews," the tremendous food shortage, the horrible vermin, the debilitating diseases and the despicable, unsanitary and crowded living conditions. Underlying all these comments, of course, is the consensus of how "lucky" we all were – despite those conditions.

Other readers were amazed to learn about "us" (Shanghailanders). There is still a big world out there that never heard that over 18,000 refugees from Nazi-occupied Europe actually survived in far-off China. At my lectures and book signings there is usually a look of disbelief.

Following are some excerpts of letters I received from third- and fourth-graders who had heard my story:

Double thank you for showing us your mother's passport and your class picture...

Thank you for coming to our school. I learned a lot. I am happy you survived. I learned it was started by Hitler and it took place in Germany...

Thank you for coming to talk to us about your experiences in the Holocaust. It was very sad to hear all about all of the terrible things that you had to go through. My Grandpa is a Holocaust survivor too...

Thank you for coming to our school and telling us about the Holocaust. Everyone learned an important lesson about the Holocaust. We learned that it was very hard for the Jews and we suffered a lot. If we forget about the Holocaust it might happen again and that would be horrible. But after what you said, I don't think that anybody at our school will forget the Holocaust...

I would just like to say thank you. I've never met any other person with such a colorful past. Since I'm not a Jew, I heard very little about Hitler

Also, since the 1994 publication of GHETTO SHANGHAI, our family has grown. My husband Lenny and I are now the proud grandparents of fourteen wonderful grandchildren – ten girls and four boys.

At the end of my lectures I am usually asked whether I have ever returned to Shanghai or to Breslau. Having taken these two trips in 1995 and 1997 respectively, I have included in this **Addendum** a short description of my impressions of these visits, which I hope the reader will find illuminating and interesting, particularly the connection to my roots in a Europe where the Nazis had planned their Final Solution.

Evelyn Pike Rubin
Jericho, New York
November 2000

SHANGHAI 1995

One year after publication of GHETTO SHANGHAI, I returned to the city I had grown up in - the city of my survival - accompanied by my husband. As the China Northwest Airbus descended for landing, my emotions took over. I remembered a different arrival, with my parents, fifty-six years earlier, on the "*Hakozaki Maru*," traveling on a German passport emblazoned with the Nazi swastika, a big red "J" and "Sara" as my middle name – and we had no departure date. Now I was carrying an American passport, I did not have to use "Sara" as my middle name, and I had a departure date. I was a visitor, not a refugee.

As I looked out the window, I started to cry. It suddenly hit me that I was close again to my father and to my grandmother. They never made it out of Shanghai, yet, I could not help thinking, at least they died a "natural" death. Even though my father was a victim of Buchenwald and died at the young age of 43, neither he, nor my grandmother ended up in the ovens of the Nazi crematoria. I thought of my mother who had the fortitude to get all of us to Shanghai. And, again, I thought of myself as a "lucky" survivor.

We had been invited to stay with Tess Johnston, secretary to the American Consul in Shanghai, and the unofficial PR person for Americans visiting that area. When I queued up for a taxi to take us to her apartment on *Huai Hai Lu* – Avenue Joffre to me, instinctively, it came to me, no one queues up – you push your way to the front of the line! Within less than five minutes I had a taxi.

Nothing looked familiar. No one wore Chinese clothes. Everyone wore western dress. No one spoke English, or even pidjin English, the lingua franca of the Shanghai I grew up in.

Prof. Pan Guang, of the Center for Jewish Studies, had invited me to give a talk. I was warmly welcomed by about a half dozen Chinese professors of the Shanghai Academy for Social Studies. Within the last decade there has been much interest in "our story," and many articles and pamphlets had been published in the Chinese press, both in English and Chinese, about the life and survival of the 18,000 or so refugees. Also included was research done by Prof. Pan Guang and others, on the Baghdadi and Russian Jewish immigration, and, going even further back, on the Kaifeng Jews.

iv

This Shanghai Jewish Studies Association prides itself on having established special classes to teach about Judaism and Israel.

(In 1997, Prof. Pang Guang came to my home in Jericho with a professional camera crew to film my family and present life style. The idea was to tell the story of the life of the refugees during the war and the new life they created after liberation. My story is just one of many.)

I inquired about the subject that was so close to my heart and the main reason I had returned to Shanghai – the "relocation" of the Jewish cemeteries.

There was an uncomfortable silence, until I realized that the professor in charge of the Shanghai Department of Cemeteries was the only one in the room who did not speak English, and my inquiry, as well as his remarks, had to be translated. What I could gather was that during the Cultural Revolution, four of the then existing "foreign" cemeteries – three Jewish and one Christian – were either moved, possibly to one of the surrounding suburbs of Shanghai, or destroyed.

At the end of my lecture, Huang Ming Xin, the director of Shanghai TV, approached me. He offered to translate GHETTO SHANGHAI into Chinese for distribution in China.

The following day we set off with an old map of Shanghai and Henry Hong our guide/interpreter. We walked up *Huai Hai Lu*, Avenue Joffre, to the compound at 1817A. When we arrived at a double size green gate with the number 1813 on it, we knocked; we were let into a small courtyard from where we could only see a wall. The tree-lined lane, that I remembered so vividly, was nowhere in sight. We were told that the rest of the property consisted of a military compound. When we tried to walk through the gate, the soldier, who was guarding the entrance, adamantly refused to even let me take a peek past the entrance. That took care of my vision of visiting my pre-ghetto home and the little synagogue, which undoubtedly no longer existed, where I had said *Kaddish* for my father.

Our next stop was the Shanghai Jewish School. There, too, we got only as far as the courtyard – the guard would not let us go further. I saw my old school building, which now houses municipal offices. What used to be our playground and hockey field is now cemented over. An apartment building and other tall buildings are in its place. The synagogue was still there – overgrown with ivy. From the outside, it looked undamaged but uncared for. We were not allowed in, and advised that it would be refurbished as a museum.

(When President Clinton visited Shanghai, he was allowed to enter the synagogue where renovations had already begun.)

An apartment house was in the process of being constructed on the site of RIPO Typewriters.

I was now on The Bund, which I remembered well, even though the area has been totally modernized. At the *Huang Pu* (Whangpoo) River's edge there is now a beautiful promenade. As I walked to the old wharf where we had arrived from Europe in 1939 and from which we had departed for the United States in 1947, I distinctly remembered that arrival and departure.

And now we were crossing the Garden Bridge into *Hongkou*, Hongkew – the area of the wartime ghetto. I half-expected to see the Japanese soldiers with their rifle and raised bayonet standing on both sides of the bridge, in their little booth. But, of course, they were long gone. The trolley, cyclists and pedestrians, crossed the bridge unimpeded. Henry Hong hailed a cab and we stopped at what used to be the ghetto entrance.

Not much had changed, except there was now an overpass where the movie theatre used to be, that had served as our synagogue for Rosh Hashanah and Yom Kippur services. Ghoya's offices, where we had stood in line for our "Special Pass" was being torn down to make room for an office building.

The Ohel Moshe synagogue, on *Chang Yang Lu* (we had always called it the "Ward Road shul"), now housed educational offices on the ground floor while refugee memorabilia – carefully and lovingly supervised by Mr. Wang – was displayed on the first floor, in a mini-museum setting.

As we walked out, we came upon a little park from which I could see the buildings of the former Ward Road *Heim* – the dormitories where so many of the refugees had been quartered. In the middle of the park, in a floral setting, there was a little plaque in Chinese, English and Hebrew with the following inscription:

THE DESIGNATED AREA FOR STATELESS REFUGEES

From 1937 to 1941, thousands of Jews came to Shanghai fleeing from Nazi persecution. Japanese occupation authorities regarded them as "stateless refugees" and set up this designated area to restrict their residence and business. The designated area was bordered on the west by Gongping Road, on the east by Tongbei Road, on the south by Huiming Road, and on the North by Zhoujiazui Road.

Hongkou District People's Government

I was very touched seeing this memorial. At least we would not be forgotten.

Immediately, we were surrounded by some of the inhabitants of the area. They were very excited when Henry explained to them who I was and many remembered the refugees who had lived in the area. They were most friendly and welcoming.

Across the street was the Ward Road jail where many of us had taken refuge during strafings by American warplanes. Next-door was the former prison hospital that had housed numerous American and British POW's. I was tempted to stop and wave, as I had done so many years ago to the POW's as they stood on the balconies. It is now an apartment house. The street itself looked almost unchanged. The "lanes" were still there, but we did not see bodies of half-starved men, women and children lying in the gutter. Almost everyone we encountered was pretty well dressed.

We proceeded to No. 498 – the entrance to my ghetto home. The front of the lane looked the same.

"Where are the hot water stands?" I wondered.

But of course they were long gone, replaced by a little booth where people could pay their electric bills. We turned into the first little alley, totally unchanged, narrow, dank and dusty; and now I was standing in front of No. 8 – the number written on the brick in white chalk. The door was open, the entrance unlit. Henry walked in and a young man appeared. He explained to him that I was one of the former tenants who had lived there during the war.

Immediately, his face broke out in a smile and he beckoned us to come in. I looked for the horrible toilet with the huge red spiders crawling around that we had installed in 1943. That was gone. I walked up the dark, wooden stairs – the stairs on which the house cat would present us with a little mouse in its jaws almost every morning. I was actually looking for the scampering cockroaches that luckily, were nowhere to be seen.

As we were standing in front of the door of the room in which my mother and I had lived during the ghetto years until our departure in 1947, time stood still. It was 1943 again; we had just moved from the French Concession into this little space, smaller than most closets.

I held my breath, as the door was unlocked for us. It was now an artist's studio.

"Was the room really so small?" I muttered to myself, while my husband just stared.

"You lived in there?" he asked.

"Yes, we lived in there. I can't believe it myself," I answered.

In the meantime, the other tenants appeared. They were warm and very friendly and insisted I look over all the rooms and take photographs. The only difference in the rooms was the furniture, the television sets and cell phones!

I went up to the roof from where we had done our cooking on the little stove that had to be fanned to keep the fire going. It looked exactly the same.

As we returned to the main lane, a lady appeared and pointed at me. She said she remembered me and described my mother perfectly! However, she indicated that I had been much thinner! (It must have been during my malnutrition days.)

The following day we set out on our own. Armed with a map and an English-Chinese transliterated dictionary, we took the subway.

(This was something new; there had been no subway when I lived there.)

Everyone was most helpful giving us directions as we made our way to the site of the Columbia Road cemetery, where my father was buried in 1941. We proceeded down a narrow lane, on either side of which there were some very small houses, almost like huts. We encountered many curious, but definitely not unfriendly stares, as we were the only westerners in that area.

Suddenly, I came across a gravestone that had been used as a paving stone, with a *Magen David*, Jewish Star, a name and a date of death sometime in 1942. Now I knew I was in the right place!

"Would I find my father's stone?" I was wondering.

We walked further and saw a similar gravestone right in front of the entrance of one of the little huts. Just as I was about to take a photograph, a lady came out of the house and gestured to me that I should wait a moment. She then re-appeared with a pail of water and washed down the stone, so that I could get a better picture. What a beautiful and sensitive gesture.

It occurred to me that all of the paving stones were probably gravestones from that cemetery that had been turned over, and the two I saw had been left that way by accident. I then knew that one of the stones I was walking on was probably that of my father, even though I never found his stone. However, I stopped and said *Kaddish*, the Jewish prayer for the dead, and departed.

Next, we went searching for the former Point Road cemetery where my grandmother was buried. A friendly cab driver, to whom I explained, using my little dictionary, what I was looking for, found the site, now a cement factory!

On the last day of our visit, we stopped at *Rinmin* Park at People's Square – the former Racecourse where I had won all my ribbons. There was no resemblance to the Racecourse, but instead a beautiful, spotless park was in its place. As we were walking around the park, we heard a voice behind us:

"Excuse me, excuse me, are you American?"

As we turned around we saw an elderly gentleman running to catch up with us. It turned out, he wanted to practice his English, which, he informed us, he had learned by watching television. As a matter of fact, on many occasions we met high school students who were also anxious to converse with us.

As we left Shanghai, I felt that I was leaving my father and grandmother again. For a little while, I had felt I was with them. I was going home to America and they will, forever, remain in the dust of the distant Orient.

BUDAPEST 1997

Budapest is a beautiful city, which had at one time a vibrant Jewish community. We took a tour around the Jewish area, which included the former ghetto and the restored Dohany Street synagogue. The little museum next door contains beautiful artifacts depicting all the Jewish holidays. Adjacent to the building is the Wallenberg Garden. The memorial to the six million murdered Jews is a weeping willow tree, which is also an inverted menorah. Each of the silver leaves bears the name of a murdered Hungarian Jew!

On the Sabbath, we attended services at the synagogue, which was described to us as a "neolog" service. Even though men and women sit separately, a fourteen-person choir performs at special Sabbath services and all Yom Tov services, accompanied by an organ. The synagogue's 250 Torahs had been hidden from the Nazis by a priest and returned to their rightful place in the ark after liberation.

It was interesting to note that most of the worshippers at this Sabbath service were tourists. This synagogue has been described as one of the most beautiful in Europe. I will certainly agree. It is magnificent. It is also the world's second largest, seating 3,000 people, (Temple Emanuel in New York is the largest, seating 3,500.)

In the Castle district, we discovered the restored remains of a medieval synagogue.

As we visited the Hungarian Museum of History, I was hoping to see mention of Raoul Wallenberg, the Swedish diplomat who had saved the lives of thousands of Hungarian Jews by providing them with false papers and hiding them in "safe" houses. In a small corner reserved for Holocaust history, we found a photograph of Wallenberg as swell as several photos of the Iron Guard, as they were shooting the Jews they were able to round up, before the Russians entered Budapest. There was also a graphic picture of them throwing their bodies into the Danube.

A statue to Raoul Wallenberg can be found in a residential district on the outskirts of the city. At the end of hostilities, he was arrested by the Soviets when they entered Budapest. No one has heard of him since!

AUSCHWITZ 1997

Shortly after our arrival in Cracow by overnight train from Budapest, we drove our rental car on a well-paved and well-marked road to the most infamous of death camps. I wanted to pay my respects to all my murdered relatives. When I saw the road marker with an arrow pointing to Oswiecim, it sent shivers up and down my spine.

Walking through the gate marked *Arbeit Macht Frei,* numbness set in. The world stopped as a feeling of unreality engulfed me.

I kept my distance from the many tour groups, for I didn't want to hear the guides' rehearsed spiel. I needed to be alone. Alone with my thoughts! The barbed wire, with their ludicrous signs, *Vorsicht! Hochspannung!* Careful, High Voltage! sent tremors through my body. Walking through just two of the buildings was enough for me.

As I stood in front of the ovens in the Crematorium, I thought I was in a Twilight Zone. I imagined my uncle Leo, who was transported to Auschwitz from France in 1942, ending up in that oven. What kind of human beings were able to undertake this horror of shoving people into gas chambers, into ovens, men, women, little children.

There was nothing to say, except the *Kaddish* prayer for my uncle Leo, for my cousin Ruben, who had been deported with him, and for everyone else who had perished there.

We proceeded to Birkenau, approximately one mile from the concentration camp. I visualized the march that these poor souls were forced to take to their death. And, here, we were driving on a beautiful road, lined with trees and pretty flowers, up to the entrance right next to the infamous railroad tracks.

Beyond the tracks, from the watchtower, we saw miles and miles of green grass. Every few hundred feet a chimney stuck out. After walking through one of the barracks, where people had been crammed into little wooden bunks, I was unable to continue. I could go no further.

With tears streaming down my face, like a broken record, over and over again I heard myself saying, "If Mutti hadn't gotten the tickets to Shanghai, that's where we would have ended up!"

WROCLAW 1997

It was only a four-hour drive from Cracow to Wroclaw, which I had always known as Breslau, but it might just as well have been a million miles away. After Auschwitz, it was a haunting experience to enter the city on *ul. Powstancow Slaskich*, which I had always known as the Kaiser Wilhelmstrasse. I could almost see the Nazis parading down that avenue even though it was now an all-Polish city.

"Have I returned to my roots?" I wondered aloud.

Ironically, our hotel was on that street, just a block away from *ul. Zielinskiego*, Höfchenstrasse, where I was born. I tried to get a feel of the city when I checked into the hotel. When I inquired of the receptionist which language was easier for her – English or German – I was told either one would be okay. I opted for English.

I was anxious to make conversation. After all, this was the city where, my parents had lived so happily, where I was born, started school and had so many friends. As I handed over my American passport which, of course, lists the country of my birth as Germany, I mentioned that this was the first time, in fifty-eight years, that I had returned to the city of my birth, after fleeing the Nazis in 1939. There was no reaction. I might as well have discussed the weather with her!

The next morning we drove to No. 9 *ul. Wlodkowica*, Wallstrasse, the location of the *Storch* synagogue where I had worshipped, as a child, with my parents. It was also now the location of the *Gmina Wyznaniowa Zydowska*, the Jewish Community Center.

There was a note posted on the door that Yiddish, German and English speakers are available to deal with visitors. We entered one of the offices where I inquired about *Friedhof* Cosel – the cemetery where three of my grandparents were buried – the reason for visiting Wroclaw. It had always been my mother's wish to visit the cemetery once again. She was never able to do so, therefore, I had taken it upon myself to fulfill her wish. The last time I had been at this cemetery was with my parents, in February 1939, just before our departure for Shanghai.

I had in my possession the family records listing the burial sites and grave numbers for my grandparents. I was astonished, when the president of the Center produced a log of burials at Cosel dating from 1928, which listed, among others, my grandmother Miriam Nelken's name as well as that of my grandfather Sally Popielarz. (My grandfather Avrohom Nelken had died in 1911 and therefore was not listed in the log.)

Imagine my disappointment to be informed, that though the cemetery had been left intact when the Nazis were driven out after the surrender, much of the cemetery had subsequently been vandalized, including the area of my grandparents' graves. Despite this information, I still wanted to go to the cemetery and see this destruction for myself. Mr. Kaszen, who spoke German, called the caretaker to meet us there.

We drove to *Friedhof* Cosel, and to my consternation, were greeted by a profusion of big, white splotches of paint on the imposing brick wall on either side of the beautiful, wrought iron gate. I was informed that the paint covered up anti-Semitic graffiti!

We walked through the cemetery with Mr. Kaszen, following the Polish caretaker, through a virtual jungle of overgrown plants and bushes, broken pieces of toppled gravestones, and almost total devastation. All the granite gravestones had disappeared. There was nothing left – only a jungle. Even the Heroes Monument, dedicated to the many Jewish soldiers who had died for the fatherland during the First World War, had been vandalized. We were told that the German government was considering restoring it.

Again, I recited a *Kaddish* prayer at a site without seeing a grave – this time for three grandparents.

It was a very traumatic visit, which was to become even more so when we returned to the Jewish Community Center.

Behind the building, on the left of the courtyard was the synagogue. Evidently, in 1992, there had been a fire, which the Polish authorities had labeled "suspicious." Most of the interior had been destroyed and was in the process of being restored. Ironically, during the *Kristallnacht* pogrom of November 1938, the Nazis had dynamited the *Neue Synagoge*, the Reform synagogue, but had left the *Storch* intact because it was situated too close to a residential area.

I had fond memories of attending Sabbath services and celebrating the holidays at this synagogue. I ascended the marble staircase leading up to the women's balcony, and remembered sitting there with my mother while my father prayed downstairs with the men.

I closed my eyes and could still see myself walking to services with my parents, meeting and greeting friends along the way. After services, we would go home for lunch and then visit friends in their homes, or friends would come to visit us. After sundown, my father would light the twisted *Havdalah* candle and we would sniff the spice box as it was passed around. It was a beautiful silver spice box with an intricate design, which looked like silver lace. I often wondered what the Nazis did with it after we had to deliver it to them with all our other valuables.

On *Yom Kippur*, Marta, my nanny, used to come to that courtyard with a *Brötchen* for me, for girls under twelve years of age and boys under thirteen did not have to fast.

On *Simchat Torah*, the holiday celebrating the completion of the year's Torah reading, we used to dance in the courtyard with the Torahs, and the children paraded with their flags. However, with much bitterness, I also recalled how we had to hide the flag from the Nazis when walking home, by wrapping it in brown paper.

This Sabbath, my husband and I attended services in a little prayer room where usually weekday services were conducted. The men sat in the front and the women in the back. They just about had a *minyan,* the quorum of ten men required for prayer. After services, we were most graciously invited to partake of a delicious kosher lunch.

At one time, Breslau had a population of approximately 20,000 Jews. The synagogue was always packed on the Sabbath. The present Jewish population of Wroclaw is approximately 1,500. No one is of German-Jewish origin. Most are Polish Jews who survived the Holocaust, or their children.

We took some walks around the city; I was looking for my childhood memories. But this was a different city, and all the streets that I had remembered now had Polish names. I had a map with all the old German names and tried to coordinate it with the new map.

We crossed over the *Odra* River, to *ul. Swidnicka*, Schweidnitzerstrasse, where we would shop at the Wertheimer department store which, for generations, was owned by a Jewish family till it was appropriated by the Nazis. Today, it is still a department store, now called *Centrum.* It was strange to see a McDonald sign in Polish at the entrance.

We walked to the *Ring*, a large square with many restaurants, shops and cafés. In the center there was still the original *Rathaus*, Town Hall, which I remembered visiting with my parents at various times. The surrounding buildings had all been restored.

I tried to find grandmother Miriam's apartment on Gartenstrasse. No. 8 is now a parking lot.

The Opera house, which my parents had so lovingly frequented, was still standing – unchanged.

We tried to find Lothringerstrasse, where my school as well as my parents' business had been located. All gone. When the Russians liberated the city, they razed the whole western sector.

My last stop was *Kruzca*, Charlottenstrasse, where I had spent the first eight years of my life. Part of the street was still there. I looked for No. 24 and the beautiful, tall ivy-covered apartment house. There were now some small, attached houses at that location. However, I could not find No.24 on any of them.

Even though our hotel was just a couple of blocks away from the *Hauptbahnhof*, the train station from which we had departed for Italy, I could not make myself go there. My visit was too painful.

I could feel no connection to my roots in that city. It would be in Prague, a city I had never visited before, where I would get connected.

PRAGUE 1997

Prague is a magnificent city and deserves the name "the Paris of Eastern Europe." At first, we took a ride to *Karoly Vary*, Carlsbad, where my grandmother used to go for her summer vacation to take the "baths." My mother and I would join her there for a few days every summer.

We took a walk through the historic Jewish section to visit the old cemetery and the various synagogues – all but one now serve as museums for Jewish documents and memorabilia. What a shock, to see the all the walls and the ceiling of the Pincus synagogue covered with the names of 82,000 Jews, who were deported from Czechoslovakia.

Another shock met us as we walked into the section of the museum that contained many of the letters and drawings of the 15,000 children, only one hundred of whom survived, who were deported to *Terezin* (Theresienstadt), which we had already visited. Oh, how I could relate to those letters. Written in German, it was noted that most of those murdered children were born between 1929 and 1932. My generation! Any one of these letters could have been mine – were it not for survival in Shanghai.

The highlight of this trip was going to be my visit to the Ziskov Jewish Cemetery, the burial place of my great-great-great-great-great grandfather, Ezekiel Landau and eight members of his immediate family. *Harav Hagaon* Yechezkel Halevi Landau, well known in Talmudic circles by the name of his responsa, *Noda B'Yehuda*, was Chief Rabbi of Prague from 1754 until his death in 1793. Standing in awe, at that gravesite, it occurred to me that I could finally recite a *Kaddish* prayer in a non-desecrated cemetery, while paying my respects to relatives who had died so long ago.

On the Sabbath, we attended services at the *Alt-Neu* Synagogue, a structure dating back to the fifteenth century, where the women had to sit behind a thick wall, with apertures at various places in order to hear the service conducted in the men's sanctuary. However, I still felt spiritually uplifted to be praying in a synagogue where, probably, my Landau ancestors had worshipped two centuries earlier.

I now felt that I had come full circle and discovered my roots!